Tragedy and tragicomedy
in the plays of John Webster

For Glenys

Tragedy and tragicomedy
in the plays of John Webster

Jacqueline Pearson

Barnes & Noble Books

First published in the USA
by Barnes & Noble Books,
81 Adams Drive, Totowa,
New Jersey 07512

ISBN 0 389 20030 1

Photosetting by
Northern Phototypesetting Co., Bolton
Printed in Great Britain
by Redwood Burn Limited
Trowbridge & Esher

Contents

Acknowledgements

My main academic debts are to Inga-Stina Ewbank, and to Anne Barton, who supervised the thesis in which this book originated not only with the weight of her scholarship but also with infallible tact and good humour. Errors and omissions are wholly my own. Parts of the book, in rather different form, have been read as papers at Bedford College, University of London, at Loughton College of Further Education, and at the University of Manchester, and I am grateful to those who listened for their helpful suggestions.

Introduction

There is no Elizabethan or Jacobean playwright who has provoked so much disagreement about the nature of his achievement as John Webster. Neil Carson has remarked on 'these glaringly contradictory opinions about the nature of Webster's mature art': 'What is striking about discussion of the work of John Webster is the absence of that larger area of agreement within which meaningful arguments about detail can take place. There is no universally acceptable definition of Webster's peculiar genius.'[1] One of the reasons for this is that most critics see Webster as essentially a tragedian whose later works turn out to be failed tragedies. Most of Webster's surviving plays were written in collaboration, and in many of these plays there is little sign of the Webster spirit. Even so, to focus only on two mature and independent tragedies, *The White Devil* (1612) and *The Duchess of Malfi* (1614), is to distort the shape of Webster's career and also to make these two difficult tragedies more difficult than necessary by placing them in a vacuum. What I shall try to do in this book is to examine in detail the four plays in which we can be confident of tracing Webster's hand, two tragedies and two tragicomedies, one, *The Devil's Law-case* (1617), written independently, the other, *A Cure for a Cuckold* (1625), written in collaboration with William Rowley. I shall argue that Webster's dramatic interests are in the incoherences of real life, the mixture of modes and the collision of different images and different interpretations of action; in fact that the tragicomedies, far from showing a sharp decline from the achievement of the tragedies, actually crown a remarkable career. I shall do this by tracing what seem to me to be tragicomic elements through four plays.

I intend too to discuss the structures which Webster devises in these four plays for expressing his view of the clashing opposites which make up human life. Despite work done by P. B. Murray, D. C. Gunby, Inga-Stina Ewbank, Gunnar Boklund and others, there is still relatively little criticism of Webster's tragicomedies. *A Cure for a Cuckold* especially is a neglected play, and very little criticism exists which is not primarily concerned with the play's divided authorship. Much of the criticism of the tragicomedies, moreover, is concerned with them as moral documents rather than as actable plays. I have tried to redress the balance. My view of Webster is not that of a morbid genius writing tragedies by torchlight, but of a man of the theatre whose view of the world encompassed extremes of comedy and tragedy, and who expressed these extremes in four perfectly structured plays.

No age was more aware than that of Elizabeth and James I of the clashing extremes from which life is made. In Whitney's *A Choice of Emblems* (1586) the motto 'In Vitam Humanam' is illustrated by a picture of the two philosophers Heraclitus and Democritus, the one weeping and the other laughing over the nature of human life. In John Marston's tragicomedy *Jack Drum's Entertainment* (1600), the playwright expresses this by bringing on stage two pages, 'the one laughing, the other crying'[2] for no special reason. Again and again in Webster's plays, even in the tragedies, a single episode provokes such differing reactions.

The dramatic form which organises these clashing tones most coherently is tragicomedy. I begin by looking briefly at the development of Elizabethan tragicomedy, its nature and its self-definitions (Chapter One). In Chapters Two and Three I examine formal tragicomedy, especially as practised by Marston, by Shakespeare and by Beaumont and Fletcher, and I attempt some generalisations about its nature. Jacobean tragicomedy has attracted relatively little criticism, and much of that is derogatory. Rupert Brooke saw it as a self-indulgent form which drowned the stage in 'a sea of saccharine'.[3] T. B. Tomlinson sees it as evidence of the 'decadence'[4] of the drama. Even Muriel Bradbrook has suggested that in Jacobean and Caroline drama 'the coarsening of the fibre may be seen in the blurring of the tragic and comic'.[5] I have tried to suggest positive virtues in these plays, stressing their astringent wit, their critical attention to their own conventions, and their examination of a shifting world where values, judgements, and even language become uncertain.

In Chapters Four to Eight I trace Webster's development in his search for a structure to express significant contrasts and discontinuities. I shall point out where Webster seems to be drawing from the conventions of tragicomedy, and other areas where he seems to reach the same ends by different methods.

In my investigation of tragicomic elements in Webster's plays I shall pay particular attention to play endings. There are several reasons for this. Critics of Webster very frequently direct their sharpest attacks to the endings of the plays. Una Ellis-Fermor finds *A Cure for a Cuckold* a moderately successful play 'until frivolous complications of plot and contradictions of character destroy the fifth act'.[6] Madeleine Doran has launched a similar attack on the resolution of *The Devil's Law-case*.[7] The final act of *The Duchess of Malfi* has been much attacked, by William Archer but also by later critics.[8] Even the last act of *The White Devil* has been attacked, as Flamineo acts out the fiction of his murder.

I have looked at endings especially, then, because they have attracted so much adverse criticism. I have also given them so much attention because the ending is a part of the play where the relationship between audience and play is especially under pressure. As the fiction ends, the playwright must find ways of drawing the audience from their absorption in the enacted fiction to a return to their real lives. The beginning of a play must engage us: it is often the part of the play which is richest in imagery and in word-play, as it creates the fictional world. The play ending must help us to make a disengagement. The ending might significantly include blatant improbabilities, like the happy ending of *The Threepenny Opera*, or the reported conversion of Duke Frederick in *As You Like It*, and it may also include images of art and fiction, or even a full-scale play within the play, which forms a transitional area for the audience between the play and real life. I have examined the way these play-endings use the audience, mediating for them between the play and the world. Why does Flamineo stage his own murder in *The White Devil?* Why does the Duchess of Malfi die a whole act before the end of the play? Why does the last act of *The Devil's Law-case* use so much visual, and so little verbal, explanation? Why does the last act of *A Cure for a Cuckold* move towards theatrical parody? It is with problems like this that I shall be concerned.

Part One
Background

1
'A play it is':
Elizabethan dramatic nomenclature
and the development of tragicomedy

As Allardyce Nicoll has pointed out, drama, to a greater extent than other arts, attempts to define and describe its own fictional nature. So strong is this 'steady trend towards the indication of dramatic categories'[1] that even non-dramatic works when they attempt to define themselves rely on the categories of the drama: one thinks of d'Aubigné's *Les Tragiques*, or the sub-titles of James Branch Cabell's novels.

Elizabethan dramatists especially define the fictional nature of their plays and their genres in a rich variety of ways. Included images of the theatre and of theatrical presentation are very common. This theatrical self-consciousness may express itself in the staging of a play or masque within the play, as in *A Midsummer Night's Dream* or Beaumont and Fletcher's *The Maid's Tragedy*. Again, actors may appear as dramatic characters, as they do in *Hamlet*, Massinger's *The Roman Actor*, or Brome's *The Antipodes*. Moreover unexpected characters turn out to have dabbled in amateur dramatics: Hieronimo in *The Spanish Tragedy*, Anselmo in *Mucedorus*, or Justice Shallow, who once played the part of King Arthur's fool Sir Dagonet, for instance. The playwrights give their characters a convincingly lifelike quality by presenting them as actors as well as fictional characters, and they set up piquant confusions between reality and the enacted fiction. Elsewhere the fact that they have once been actors can reveal even more of the characters involved. Volpone once acted the part of Antinous, a rôle which suggests his perverse sexuality. Julia's male persona in *The Two Gentlemen of Verona* talks of playing the part of Ariadne betrayed by Theseus, thus presenting her own situation with poignant indirection: it is a very suitable image in a play about betrayal. Finally Polonius not only is a critic of drama and of performance, but also was once an amateur actor. The fact that he once played the part of Caesar provides ironic parallels and contrasts

7

for his present situation: he has all the weakness of Shakespeare's Caesar but none of his strength, and like Caesar he is soon to be stabbed to death. By means of details like these playwrights again and again point out to us the fictional nature of the play and define its genre.

An especially interesting way in which the author carries on this discussion, particularly in plays of mixed or indeterminate genre, is the use of the induction in which characters not themselves central to the play comment on, or provide a parallel to, the action which is about to be presented. The induction was a popular device in the romantic or documentary plays of the 1580s and 1590s, and also in the satirical plays of the late 1590s and the early years of the seventeenth century, but the nature of the induction in the two cases is very different. The inductions of the early plays are largely concerned with defining tone and establishing genre. They centre on allegorical or supernatural figures who control or comment on the actions of the human characters of the play: Venus, Fortune and the Fury Tisiphone in *The Rare Triumphs of Love and Fortune* (1582), Revenge and the ghost of Andrea in *The Spanish Tragedy* (1587), Venus and the nine Muses in *Alphonsus King of Aragon* (1587), Love, Fortune and Death in *Soliman and Perseda* (1590), Oberon king of the Fairies in *James IV* (1590), Truth and Poetry in *The True Tragedy of Richard III* (1591), Homicide, Avarice and Truth in *Two Lamentable Tragedies* (1594). These characters introduce the play, sometimes quarreling over which is to have command over its events and what its genre is to be. In *Soliman and Perseda*, for example, Love, Death and Fortune appear not only in the induction but also between the acts to quarrel about their respective power. Death of course wins and dismisses his rivals:

Pack, Love and Fortune, play in Comedies;
For powerful Death best fitteth Tragedies (V.5.28–9)

The play's hesitation about genre is finally more apparent than real; it ends in tragic style with the triumph of death.

In some plays the induction even includes personified genres, like Comedy and Envy in *Mucedorus* (1590), or Comedy, History and Tragedy in *A Warning for Fair Women* (1599). At first glance the enormously popular *Mucedorus* seems to be the usual romantic comedy hotchpotch with a wandering princess, a prince disguised as a shepherd and in love with her, a murderous villain, a wild man of the woods, and a clown. This apparently simple subject-matter, however, is complicated by a lively sense of the ridiculous and by a sophisticated induction and epilogue. Envy, who appears in the prologue as the exponent of tragedy and in the epilogue as the exponent of satire, threatens Comedy with 'a tragic end' (Ind. 10). Comedy, though, insists upon her own power and integrity:

> Comedy is mild, gentle, willing for to please . . .
> Delighting in mirth, mixed all with lovely tales (Ind. 37–9)

The play may include 'tragic stuff', but it is none the less to end, like the Mechanicals' play in *A Midsummer Night's Dream*, as a 'pleasant comedy' (Ind. 70). The frame plot shows tragedy and comedy struggling for the play and ends, like Jonson's *Every Man out of his Humour*, with Envy defeated by the benign presence of the monarch.

A Warning for Fair Women uses the induction for a particularly detailed examination of genre. The play, a domestic tragedy based on fact, opens with the entrance of Tragedy and History. Each carries appropriate symbolic objects, History a drum and flag, Tragedy a knife and whip. They are quarrelling over the control of the play when Comedy enters, playing a fiddle, and the induction becomes an acrimonious dispute between Comedy and Tragedy. Neither has any real understanding of the other. To Tragedy, Comedy is invariably frivolous and silly:

> I must confess you have some sparks of wit,
> Some odd ends of old jests, scraped up together,
> To tickle shallow injudicial ears,
> . . . but slight and childish. (A2v)

To Comedy, Tragedy is nothing but ludicrously overstated melodrama:

> How some damned tyrant, to obtain a crown,
> Stabs, hangs, impoisons, smothers, cutteth throats,
> And then a Chorus too comes howling in,
> And tells us of the worrying of a cat,
> Then of a filthy whining ghost . . .
> Pure purple Buskin, blood and murder right. (A2v–A3)

Tragedy's self-definition is more serious, and she emphasises the strong emotional effect of the genre:

> I must have passions that must move the soul,
> Make the heart heavy, and throb within the bosom . . .
> Until I rap the senses from their course. (A2v)

The induction ends as History notices that 'the stage is hung with black' (A3), and she and Comedy retire, Comedy promising to return tomorrow. Tragedy appears between the acts as interpreter of the play's elaborate dumb-shows and as moral commentator. Finally Tragedy speaks the epilogue, pointing out that the genre as she understands it is essentially moral, displaying and attacking lust and sin, and has little to do with the contemporary vogue for melodramatic revenge plays:

> Perhaps it may seem strange unto you all,
> That one hath not revenged another's death,
> After the observation of such course:
> The reason is, that now of truth I sing. (K3)

The induction, then, gives two descriptions of tragedy, a mocking and a favourable, and an equally mocking description of comedy. The epilogue defines the rather unconventional documentary tragedy the author felt he was writing. Here the material which frames the action proper not only identifies the play as a tragedy but also narrows this down to define more minutely the kind of tragedy it is.

Inductions of the late 1590s and the early years of the seventeenth century move away from this kind of allegorising to present a more direct and realistic view of the contemporary theatre. Often a conventional prologue is interrupted to turn the attention of the audience to the mechanics of performance. Sometimes actors play themselves or other members of the staff of the playhouse. The Stagekeeper appears in the inductions to each of the two parts of *The Return from Parnassus* (1600, 1603), one of the players in *Wily Beguil'd* (1602), the Stagekeeper and Bookholder in *Bartholomew Fair* (1614), and the Tireman in *Jack Drum's Entertainment* (1600). The well-known actors Burbage, Condell and Lowin appear *in propria persona* in the induction to *The Malcontent* (1604). In the induction to *Antonio and Mellida* (1599) we are even allowed into the dressing room to hear the child actors talk about the play and their rôles in it. Often members of the audience are played by the actors, members of the audience who are occasionally praised for their intelligent discernment, like Cordatus and Mitis in *Every Man out of his Humour* (1599), but are more often mocked, like the audience in Webster's induction to *The Malcontent*, or the Citizen and his wife in *The Knight of the Burning Pestle* (1607).

These inductions are less exclusively concerned than the first group with establishing genre. Their primary function is to comment on the relationship of audience and play in other ways, by mirroring the real physical conditions in the playhouse, by discussing the politics of the theatrical companies, or by forestalling the hostile criticism of the audience by attacking the play first.[2] In Marston's *What You Will* (1601) the fictional audience attack the real playgoers, the actors, the playwright and the play. Before the full-scale fiction begins, the audience in the theatre finds itself watching itself, and real life is confronted by not one but two planes of illusion.

However some of these inductions are also concerned with establishing genre. In *Every Man out of his Humour* the frame plot lengthily examines the nature of comedy, especially the comedy of humours, its rules, its decorum, its history and its structure. Often, though, these plays raise questions of genre only to stress that the play is of no readily definable kind. *1 Return from Parnassus* is 'a Christmas toy' (Ind. 18), *2 Return* 'but a Christmas jest' (Ind. 58), trifles not serious enough for criticism or discussion. Webster defines *The Malcontent* only as 'a bitter play' (Ind. 42). *What You Will*, we are told, belongs to none of the genres, but is 'even *What You Will*' (II, Ind., p. 233).

The two most elaborate uses of this kind of dramatic frame[3] are Jonson's *Every Man out of his Humour* and Beaumont's *The Knight of the Burning Pestle*. Both complicate the sharp distinction between illusion and reality by placing between us and the play a fictionalised version of ourselves, idealised as in *Every Man out* or grotesquely mocking as in *Knight*: though the exclusive audience of the private theatre might well refuse to take the naïve popular theatre audience of *Knight* as a self-portrait. In both the induction spills over into the play proper. Cordatus and Mitis are always ready to interrupt the action in order to comment on it, praise it, or attack it. The Citizen and his wife in *Knight* not only comment on the play but create it, changing a play originally to be called *The London Merchant* into *The Grocer's Honour, or The Knight of the Burning Pestle*, and introducing popular theatre stereotypes, knights and giants, castles and princesses, a rhetorical ghost, and an English patriotic hero. The figures of the Citizen and his wife allow Beaumont to comment on differences between public and private theatre plays, including generic ones: where Jonson's comments on genre are expressed in long discourses, Beaumont actually dramatises them. These inductions, then, are concerned with the interplay of fiction and reality in a more general sense than the earlier group, and their interest in genre is part of this larger process.

Elsewhere playwrights explore the genres more directly, simply in the use of generic terminology. Although elsewhere Elizabethan genre-criticism is so disappointing, the playwrights fill their plays with genre terms. Even these are rarely defined in any detail: Jonson's discussion of comedy in *Every Man out of his Humour*, or the definition of tragicomedy which Fletcher appends to *The Faithful Shepherdess*, are exceptional. Writers generally assume that words like 'tragedy' or 'comedy' or 'history' need no further explanation. The preface to George Whetstone's *Promos and Cassandra* (1578) is a case in point. This two-part play, a major source of Shakespeare's *Measure for Measure*, is a tragicomedy blending scenes of fooling, agonised moral dilemmas, and narrow escapes from death, in a way which clearly resembles Fletcher's tragicomedies. We might expect the preface to describe or defend the kind of mixed genre play which Whetstone is producing. This is not quite, though, what we find. He explains first why he has written a two-part play, dividing his 'history' into 'two Comedies'.[4] He then touches briefly on the mixed nature of his play, but he does so only to attack other looser kinds of generic mixture: 'Many times, (to make mirth) they make a Clown companion with a King'.[5] The rest of the preface, however, moves away from these pressing literary questions to defend drama on moral grounds. Whetstone ends with the characteristic Renaissance defence of fiction as providing not only entertainment but also education: 'The grave matter may instruct and the pleasant delight'.[6] Whetstone, then, uses the words 'comedy' and 'history' indiscriminately for his hybrid play, discusses decorum and literary history, and defends the use of fiction on moral grounds, but nowhere does he look more closely at the genre-terms he uses so loosely, and he seems to have no sense of inconsistency in his rejection of other kinds of tragicomic synthesis.

The plays themselves use genre-terminology very widely. 'Tragedy' is very commonly used by dramatic characters to describe their situation. At the end of Marlowe's *Edward II* (1592) the defeated Isabella recognises that 'Now ... begins our tragedy' (V.6.23). 'Tragedy' is characteristically the last word of Kyd's *The Spanish Tragedy* (1587), as Revenge hales the souls of the villains to hell, where he will 'begin their endless tragedy' (IV.4.48). Vindice in *The Revenger's Tragedy* (1606) especially is aesthetically interested in the events of the play as they form a tragedy, and the play uses the word repeatedly, even attempting succinct and sardonic definitions: 'When the bad bleeds, then is the tragedy good' (III.5.205).

Shakespeare's early plays are rich in generic terminology: *Henry VI* makes much use of 'tragic', 'tragical' and 'tragedy' and *Love's Labour's Lost* of 'comedy'.[7] Later, though, genre description is most frequently used to be mocked,[8] and this is especially true of elaborate descriptions of equivocal and mixed genre. Polonius's 'tragical-comical-historical-pastoral' (*Hamlet* II.2.392) and the accounts of the Mechanicals' play in *A Midsummer Night's Dream*, 'very tragical mirth' (V.1.57), 'the most lamentable comedy' (I.2.12), are not so far from the tortuous definitions of mixed genre of some of Shakespeare's contemporaries.

Thomas Preston's *Cambyses* (1567) is described on the title-page as 'a Lamentable Tragedy, mixed full of pleasant mirth'. T. Lupton's interlude *All for Money* (1577) expresses its mixed nature in the form of two paradoxes, 'a Moral and Pitiful Comedy' (play-heading) and a 'pleasant Tragedy' (Prologue 93). Shakespeare's burlesque of such attempts at critical definition points out their cumbersomeness. As early as the 1560s these terms were rivalled by the more precise and compact 'tragical comedy' and finally 'tragicomedy'.

Although Artistotle described a kind of tragedy with a happy ending which was later to be seen as tragicomic,[9] the earliest surviving definitions of the form are Roman. The word 'tragi(co)comoedia' seems to have been coined by Plautus to describe, half-jocularly, *Amphitruo*, a play which reduces a god to a cuckolder and a hero to a cuckold before shifting focus to show the event as a mystic celebration to herald the birth of Hercules. Rather like *The Comedy of Errors*, the play surrounds comedy based on misunderstanding with a terrifying sense of impending madness and the loss of identity. Renaissance writers of and apologists for tragicomedy like Guarini could and did defend their apparently unclassical hybrid form by reference to the well-springs of classicism. English critics were perhaps rather more narrow in their views. In a famous passage Sir Philip Sidney condemns 'mongrel tragicomedy', by which he means plays which injudiciously mix kings and clowns, and 'match hornpipes and funerals'.[10] Despite the strictures of critics like Sidney and Whetstone, however, audiences continued to enjoy richly mixed plays. In Webster's *The White Devil* (1612), the Duke of Florence comments on the audience's dislike of the kind of classically single-minded plays which Sidney advocates:

My tragedy must have some idle mirth in 't,
Else it will never pass.   (IV.1.119–20)

Before Fletcher, the mixed play's tendency to define its category is particularly noticeable in four plays of the latter half of the sixteenth century, plays which are especially careful to explain their descriptions of themselves because of their consciousness that they are using unfamiliar terminology. These plays differ from others of their age not so much in kind as in the directness of their genre-descriptions. R. B.'s *Apius and Virginia* (1564), Richard Edwardes' *Damon and Pythias* (1565) and George Gascoigne's *The Glass of Government* (1575) all call themselves 'tragical comedy', and Samuel Brandon's strange play *The Virtuous Octavia* (1598) is the first in English to use the term 'tragicomedy'. All four plays are particularly liberal in their use of the various genre-terms and attempt to describe with unusual precision their mixed nature.

Although F. H. Ristine sees Tudor tragical comedy as 'a form of comedy',[11] these plays seem more aware of their links with tragedy. *The Virtuous Octavia* relates the potentially tragic story at one remove. Antony and Cleopatra never appear, and their passion and death are simply reported. The centre of the play is the poignantly controlled Octavia, Antony's wife, a character who is peripheral in Shakespeare's *Antony and Cleopatra*. Brandon's play, which insists on the necessity for control and moderation, refuses to be interested in 'tragedies' which are the result of enslavement by 'traitor passion' (2.7). Although Brandon offers no formal explanation for his use of the word 'tragicomedy,' it seems here to refer to tragic events viewed from a point of severe detachment, destructive passion undercut and criticised by a rigorous Christian stoicism.

Brandon does not explain his terminology: R. B. in *Apius and Virginia* seems unhappy with his nomenclature. Although the title-page of the 1575 edition calls the play a 'Tragical Comedy', the prologue simplifies this to 'this tragedy' (19). The play mixes farce and danger, the agony of a father who murders his beloved daughter to save her from rape, the temptation of the lustful Apius, and the lively clowning of the Vice Haphazard. The prologue announces the play's double concern as both tragedy and comedy: it deals with Virginia's 'dolour and her doleful loss', but also 'her joys at death' (Prologue 17). The play consistently undercuts the elements of tragedy. Even Virginia's death is placed at some distance from the end of the play, so that the final moments might modify its pity and fear, and it is surrounded by a detaching commentary as Memory and Fame present Virginia's escape from violation as a spiritual triumph. The lively parodic comedy of Haphazard also undercuts the play's almost tragic incidents. Moreover, the author finally distances us from the play by an admission of its purely fictional nature: the whole story of passion and pain is seen in retrospect as nothing but a dramatic re-enactment, 'this Poet's feigning here' (1025).

The other two tragical comedies of the period have more in common with comedy. George Gascoigne's heavy Calvinist prodigal-son morality play *The Glass of Government* presents itself as 'a comedy' (Prologue 21), but immediately goes on to qualify this definition: it contains for instance 'No Terence phrase' (22), for Gascoigne's purpose is a more serious one. The play distinguishes its own didactic 'true discourse' (14) from the frivolous comic 'interlude' designed only 'to make you laugh' (9). According to its title-page the play is 'A tragical Comedy so entitled, because therein are handled as well the rewards for Virtues as also the punishment for Vices'. Like the prologue, the ending of the play distances itself from conventional comedy by stressing the dark side of the tragicomic synthesis, as it describes itself as a 'woeful tragical comedy' (p. 88). The good end happily and the bad unhappily: this for Gascoigne seems to be what tragicomedy means.

Of the tragical comedies of the period it is Richard Edwardes' *Damon and Pythias*, with its last-minute rescue from death and its many comic and parodic scenes, which is closest in form to the tragicomedies written by Fletcher and his imitators. The play's prologue describes its subject matter as 'mixed with mirth and care . . . a tragical comedy' (37–8), and its title-page promises 'the most Excellent Comedy of Two the Most Faithfullest Friends'. The play certainly sees itself as a comedy but, like Gascoigne, Edwardes suggests that it is a subdued and serious comedy: the audience is warned not to expect mere frivolity, 'toys . . . in comical wise' (prologue 3–4), for the play is a 'tragical comedy' (38). The initial definition as comedy is immediately undercut. Moreover, although the prologue so clearly sees the play as a comedy of sorts, the dramatic image used most frequently in the play itself is that of tragedy. Pythias is threatened with execution, and Stephano describes his situation as 'this tragedy' (1112): later the converted tyrant Dionysius, reprieving the two friends, looks back on their courage and fidelity in the face of danger as 'this tragedy' (2131). Tragedy and comedy clash in the play:

the danger of death, a happy ending in which this is averted, and the addition of comic episodes, songs and moral debate, combine to produce 'tragical comedy'.

These four plays present little consensus of opinion about the meaning of 'tragical comedy' as a critical term. *Apius and Virginia* and *The Virtuous Octavia* include potentially tragic events, *The Glass of Government* and *Damon and Pythias* come closer to comedy. All, except the anomalous *The Virtuous Octavia*, mix noblemen and slaves and ironically set tragedy or near tragedy against parodic and deflating incidents – the irreverent commentary of the Vice Haphazard in *Apius and Virginia*, the ludicrous ill-treatment of Grim the Collier in *Damon and Pythias*, or the dangerous comedy of prostitute, bawd and bully in *The Glass of Government*. All make much use of generic terminology. All distance a basic tragic experience, sometimes by a surprising happy ending, sometimes by presenting tragedy early in the play and allowing the final scenes to modify its effect, sometimes by extensive and distancing use of debate and discussion, sometimes by an insistence on the fictional nature of what is happening. In terms of structure, though, they are very different. *The Virtuous Octavia* shows tragedy from the sidelines, *Apius and Virginia* is a moral interlude of martyrdom and punishment, *Damon and Pythias* has a main plot and sub-plot and averts at the last moment the danger of tragedy, and *The Glass of Government* has a double plot and shows a heavily moral judgement on the frivolity of comedy.

Nor is there more unanimity in other dramatic uses of words like 'tragicomical' or 'tragical comedy'. In 1591 the second quarto of Lyly's *Campaspe* calls the play a 'tragical comedy'. Comedy usually ends with the marriage of the hero and heroine: in Lyly's play Alexander gives up the woman he loves so that she might marry Apelles. Alexander chooses his public duty before his private inclination, electing to 'command himself' (1611) and thereby 'command the world' (1610–11). A comedy, the play nonetheless throws out of focus the final comic moment. *Soliman and Perseda* (1590) also makes much use of generic description, calling itself a 'tragedy' (I.1.17, 27, 36, II.1.261, IV.3.18, V.2.140), but also a 'history' (IV.3.17), and it even uses the words 'Comedy' (V.2.141, V.4.7) and 'tragicomical' (V.2.143). The sultan Soliman loves Perseda, the wife of his friend Erastus, and to get her he has her husband murdered. Soliman congratulates himself on the happiness which is in store for him, but he is also uncomfortable:

Here ends my dear Erastus' tragedy,
And now begins my pleasant Comedy;
But if Perseda understand these news,
Our scene will prove but tragicomical. (V.2.140–3)

Erastus's fate was a 'tragedy' because it ended in death, Soliman's a 'comedy' because he hopes it will end in marriage and happiness. However this 'comedy' is precarious: if Perseda realises Soliman's guilt his happy ending will never take place. Here 'tragicomical' suggests a happiness which may at any moment tip over into disaster.

Again, Ben Jonson's *Epicoene* (1609) also talks about tragicomedy. Truewit in a rather malicious comic spirit foments strife between Daw and La-Foole, although rather as in *Twelfth Night* both men are really too cowardly to fight. Truewit with characteristic zest promises that 'here will I act such a tragicomedy between the Guelphs and the Ghibellines, Daw and La-Foole' (IV.5.30–1). Truewit's drama is a tragicomedy because the participants are terrified but the observers 'laugh'd . . . most comically' (IV.5.6). Different viewpoints produce clashing tones, and a comic situation gives rise to disturbing jokes about real maiming.

Finally Sir William Alexander's Senecan pastiche *The Tragedy of Croesus* (1604) also makes much use of equivocal generic terminology. Solon soliloquises on the precarious state of man, an 'unreasonable reasonable creature' (11) who 'would act a comic scene of tragic life' (16). Harpagus describes Cyrus's meteoric rise to power, exposed as a baby to die but now king, as a 'tragicomic course' (2166). Later a similar description is used in the same way to refer to a movement from the danger of death to reprieve: Croesus is dragged out to execution but is finally spared, 'A tragic entry to a comic end' (2864). In these very different plays tragicomedy is given very different meanings: a fortunate situation which tips over into disaster, as in *Soliman and Perseda*, or a potentially tragic situation which nevertheless reaches a happy ending, as in *Croesus*, or a comedy which reaches a slightly off-key ending, like *Campaspe*, or a situation where widely different reactions are produced from audience and participants, as in *Epicoene*.

The plays of the period, then, show a marked lack of unanimity about what constitutes tragical comedy. They even view their own critical terminology with widely differing seriousness: Alexander uses it solemnly, Jonson mocks it. No really useful critical definition by an English playwright appeared, though, until the preface of John Fletcher's first tragicomedy, *The Faithful Shepherdess* (1608). This highly patterned, sexually explicit, fantastic pastoral tragicomedy had proved a disastrous box-office failure and Fletcher, with uncharacteristically Jonsonian asperity, rounds on his audience:

It is a pastoral tragicomedy, which the people seeing when it was played, having ever had a singular gift in defining, concluded to be a play of country hired Shepherds, in grey cloaks, . . . sometimes laughing together, and sometimes killing one another: And missing whitsun ales, cream, wassail and morris-dances, began to be angry . . . A tragicomedy is not so called in respect of mirth and killing, but in respect it wants deaths, which is enough to make it no tragedy, yet brings some near it, which is enough to make it no comedy . . .

For the first time in English Fletcher suggests that there is such a thing as a tragicomic structure, and that the form is not simply a modification of tragedy or of comedy, or the ironic articulation of plots of different kinds. Giambattista Guarini had insisted that the tragicomic structure was 'mixed' and not 'double'.[12] Fletcher simplifies Guarini to reject some Tudor ideas about tragicomedy. *Apius and Virginia* would be rejected because it mixes 'mirth and killing', and *The Glass of Government* because its effect is double rather than integrated, although *Damon and Pythias* would fit quite happily into the Fletcherian mould. Fletcher's critical stand is closer to Sidney's than might at first appear: Fletcher also rejects plays which match hornpipes and funerals and prefers a more even mixture. The importance of Fletcher's definition, rudimentary though it is, would seem to be that it would no longer be enough to define tragicomedy simply in terms of colliding tones: tragicomedy, like tragedy or comedy, had a particular and definable structure and series of images.

Until 1608, then, there was little unanimity in English about the nature of tragical comedy or tragicomedy, except for the obvious recognition of its mixed nature. It might ironically juxtapose violent death and comedy routines, like *Apius and Virginia*, or reach a happy ending despite the danger of death, like *Damon and Pythias*. The word tragicomic is used to define a tone or a collision of tones as it does in *Epicoene*, or a structure, as in *The Tragedy of Croesus*. A tragicomedy might include and refocus a tragedy, like *The Virtuous Octavia*, or present itself as a kind of comedy, like *The Glass of Government*. By 1598, though, the allegiance to tragedy of *The Virtuous Octavia* must have seemed somewhat anachronistic. Fletcher's view of tragicomedy firmly suggests a form that is unlike tragedy in kind, but unlike comedy only in degree, reaching a happy ending despite the danger of death. The preface to *The Faithful Shepherdess* attempts to define a tragicomic structure and to give the form some critical authority, and Fletcher's theory and practice are central to the development of Jacobean tragicomedy. Nonetheless, the plays of the early seventeenth century continue to be influenced by the other, older but less critically respectable, form of tragical comedy: the mixture of 'mirth and killing' shapes not only Fletcher's own play *The Two Noble Kinsmen*, but also *King Lear* and *The White Devil*.

2

'Beginning mournfully and ending merrily': the development of Jacobean tragicomedy

In 1608 John Fletcher offered a critical definition of tragicomedy. He and his collaborator Francis Beaumont, however, were far from alone in their attempts to accommodate the Tudor mixed form to a more sophisticated, disillusioned age. Shakespeare, for instance, both influenced the movement toward tragicomedy and was influenced by it. From his earliest plays his tendency is to blur the dividing lines between the genres, to juxtapose comedy with tragedy or to elicit a surprising pathos from a comic moment. In the last act of *Love's Labour's Lost* comedy dissolves as Mercade brings disturbing news from the real world. The death of the Princess's father causes the audience and the characters involved to refocus their view of the world and redefine their feelings. Finally the very triviality or aggressiveness of comedy that had previously seemed so delightful now appears only an evasion.

It is in later comedies, though, that formal tragicomedy becomes an important part of Shakespeare's effect. The romances, and especially *Cymbeline* and *The Winter's Tale*, show a clear kinship with Fletcher's tragicomedies with their strong-minded heroines, slander, separation and return from apparent death. The dark comedies also seem consciously tragicomic. *Measure for Measure* and *All's Well that Ends Well* use dense satirical detail and raise serious problems of sexual morality but nonetheless reach happy endings with marriages and reconciliation. The last act of *Measure for Measure* includes or promises four different marriages but only one, that between Claudio and Juliet, is actually welcomed by both partners. Happy ending and reconciliation are menaced by disturbing silences: Angelo says nothing to his new wife, almost nothing indeed in the last scene except twice to beg for death, the resurrected Claudio says nothing. Most disturbing, Isabella has very little to say – no words for Claudio (her last words to

him in the play are "'tis best thou diest quickly"[1]), and no answer for
the Duke's repeated proposal of marriage. This dark play finally
reaches a happy ending, but it is a peculiarly uncomfortable and
unconsoling one, solving none of the problems of the play, and
undermined by the silence of so many of the participants.

As in Shakespeare's plays, from the 1590s there were two distinct
kinds of tragicomedy: Fletcher's form, solidly based on romantic
comedy, and Marston's form which is based on satirical comedy. John
Marston, who had begun his literary career with verse satires, took
some of the materials of romance but gave a heavily satirical slant to
his disguised dukes, wicked usurpers, hyperbolic conflicts of love and
friendship, and last-minute reprieves from death. Marston specialised
in writing for the companies of child-actors where acting style seems to
have made much use of parody and burlesque, and for whom this
combination of romance and satire was consequently particularly well-
suited.[2]

Jack Drum's Entertainment (1600) is a typical play in its use of
schematic antitheses and clashing tones. In the middle of the first act,
when the gallants have been introduced, the basic antithesis between
the virtuous and the wanton daughters has been established, and both
tragedy and comedy have been suggested by the figures of the sinister
usurer Mamon and the grotesque sensualist John fo de King, two
unnamed pages suddenly enter, 'the one laughing, the other crying'
(III, p. 91):

> *Page 1.*   Why dost thou cry?
> *Page 2.*   Why dost thou laugh?
> *Page 1.*   I laugh to see thee cry.
> *Page 2.*   And I cry to see thee laugh.

This scene seems included specifically to define the mixed nature of the
play and the divided response which it expects from its audience. *Jack
Drum's Entertainment* includes attempts at murder and mutilation,
temporary and permanent madness, and grotesque violence and
sexuality. Its scenes of romantic love and pain, danger and cruelty,
though, are set against inserted songs, a farcical plot about cuckoldry,
and comic anecdotes, and the whole is pervaded by the spirit of
burlesque. Antithetical tones and incidents are arranged to comment
on each other. One page laughs and the other cries. Sir Edward
Fortune's heavily cheerful response to the mysterious disappearance of
his daughter contrasts absolutely with the passionate emotions of the

young lovers: 'Let's sing, drink, sleep, for that's the best relief' (III, p. 206). This structure of opposites is a central aspect of Jacobean tragicomedy. Although Guarini suggested that the tragicomic structure was to be a single 'mixed' plot rather than a double plot, this single plot can be complicated by an elaborate array of contrasts and double-images.

From his earliest satirical poems Marston's work is full of this arrangement of clashing tones. Again and again he insists on his divided intention and the divided response he expects from his audience. *The Metamorphosis of Pygmalion's Image* (1598) he sees as both an erotic poem and an attack on erotic poems, and this richly ambiguous use of convention is extended in his later works: the two parts of *Antonio and Mellida*, for instance, include both a revenge tragedy and a burlesque of revenge tragedy. In his second collection of satirical poems, *The Scourge of Villainy* (1598), he describes himself as writing 'in serious jest, and jesting seriousness' (Proemium in librum tertium, 1), his impulses both 'rage' and 'sporting merriment' (Satire XI, 239–240). Marston's ambivalences, though, are wider than his definitions of genre and his ironic juxtaposition of tones: he is sometimes painfully tentative about his own ability and about the value of writing satire. Even the satirical impulse itself, and its tool the literary figure of the satirist, seem questionable, 'frantic, foolish, bedlam mad' (Satire X, 10). Again and again he adds tentative disclaimers to poems and plays: 'The best best seal of wit is wit's distrust' (*What You Will*, Induction p. 233), 'He that knows most knows most how much he wanteth' (*The Malcontent*, Epilogus 18). The complex and tentative nature of his work is stressed also by his use of ironic dedications, 'To the World's Mighty Monarch, Good Opinion', 'To his most esteemed and best beloved Self', 'To everlasting Oblivion', 'To Detraction'.[3] Confidence and self-distrust clash across poems and plays, another aspect of their tissue of contrasts.

The satirical poems have a rich sense of alternate possibilities. When in 1599 Marston turned to the stage he brought with him what he had learned from these satires. The importation of character-types from the satires is one of the most obvious of these continuities: Castilio in *Antonio and Mellida*, for instance, originates in *The Scourge Of Villainy* (Satire III). The plays also elaborate on the poems' statements of divided response and divided intentions, and Marston repeatedly stresses their mixed character. The genre-term he uses most often is 'comedy', but this seems often to be simply a general term for a dramatic representation. *Jack Drum's Entertainment* is introduced as a 'Comedy' (III, p. 179), in *The Malcontent* the introductory epistle introduces 'this comedy' (27), and even the induction to that Janus-faced tragedy *Antonio and Mellida* prepares for 'this comedy' (135). This latter play, indeed, is full of clashing generic descriptions. Marston first defines his aim, to be 'seriously fantastical' (Dedication, 6), and then elaborates on this. The first part of *Antonio and Mellida* is 'this comedy' (Induction 135), 'this love's comedy' (V.1.66), 'the comic crosses of true love' (V.2.264). At the same time tragedy remains a real possibility. The last act includes 'tragedy' (V.2.215), a 'tragic spectacle' (V.2.173) in which the supposedly dead Antonio is brought in in a coffin before rising to be reunited with Mellida. The second play in the unit, *Antonio's Revenge*, makes less ambiguous genre-claims: it is 'a sullen tragic scene' (Prologue 7) 'Tragoedia Cothurnata' (II.5.45), 'some black tragedy' (V.6.63). Even here, though, the tragic potential is disturbed by a curious combination of understatement and overstatement, and by the parodic participation of the fool 'Sir' Jeffrey Balurdo in the murder of Piero. The two plays form a unique tragicomic unit, including farce and murder, tragedy and comedy. Ironic contrasts are made not only between the two parts, but even within the same unit.

Very often Marston simply refuses to apply to his plays the conventional distinctions between tragedy and comedy. *What You Will* is not 'Comedy, Tragedy, Pastoral, Moral, Nocturnal or History . . . but even *What You Will*' (II, p. 233). It seems a very slight play, based on disguise and cross-courtship, but it is given substance by its dense satirical detail, its ambivalence about the value of satire, and by a vivid terror behind the farcical incidents. Again, the prologue to *The Dutch Courtesan* repeatedly calls itself simply a play, 'this easy play' (1), 'our play' (12). Finally *The Malcontent* makes an even richer series of claims to a mixed nature. It is a play of usurpation, disguise and violence, but these are set against a satirical background of parody and ironic deflation. In the dedicatory epistle *The Malcontent* is described as a 'comedy', in Webster's induction as 'a bitter play . . . neither satire nor moral, but the mean passage of a history' (42–4). Finally in the Stationers' Register for 1604 it is described as a 'Tragicomedia'.

Marston the playwright for the select audiences of the children's theatre on the whole rejects the traditional genre-distinctions of the public playhouse and attempts to formulate new generic terms, neutral or explicitly mixed. The plays are full of images of audience and play in which the mixed genre of the play as well as its fictional nature can be explored – inductions, plays within plays, discussions of the nature of drama. *Histriomastix* (1599), as the title suggests, is among other things an attack on the incompetence and the lack of education of the authors and actors of the public theatre. It includes an enacted play, a brief and plotless hotchpotch of romantic tragedy and prodigal son morality. As the feeble playwright Posthast grotesquely muddles terms, Marston parodies the simplifying genre-distinctions of the public theatre: '*Mother Gurton's Needle* (a Tragedy); *The Devil and Dives* (a Comedy)' (III, p. 265). Again in *What You Will* the primary play is defined by contrast with two plays which are offered for presentation before the Duke of Venice. Like the hedonistic duke, Marston's play rejects both the 'moral play', the 'comedy, entitled *Temperance*' (II, p. 290), and the 'tragic solid passion' of the death of Cato (p. 291). The play refuses both morality and tragedy and gives instead a 'happy, comical' (p. 293) ending to the highly-charged plot of mistaken identity. It remains *What You Will*, but other tones are always possible, even into the last act.

Where Marston's plays approach tragicomedy through satire, those of Francis Beaumont and John Fletcher approach it through romantic comedy. Both kinds of tragicomedy blend the two – E. M. Waith has described tragicomedy as created by the interaction of satire and romance[4] – but they begin from different directions. The Fletcherian tragicomedies are unlike romantic comedy only in degree: their blend of love and the danger of death is not entirely unlike that of *A Midsummer Night's Dream* or *Much Ado about Nothing*. The plays are full of the archetypes of romantic comedy, distant and exotic settings, royal and aristocratic characters, unjust tyrants, forced marriages, girls disguised as page-boys, misunderstandings and cross-wooings and, most important, the danger of death averted, the quality which in the preface of *The Faithful Shepherdess* Fletcher sees as defining tragicomedy. Death, of course, is averted in *A Midsummer Night's Dream* or *As You Like It*, but Fletcher is concerned in making this escape more central, more difficult, and more clearly surrounded by colliding tones. In *A Midsummer Night's Dream*, for instance, Hermia is threatened with death if she refuses to marry Demetrius, but we are never seriously afraid that this will happen: the danger of death remains simply as a poignant disturbance of the perfection of human happiness. In Fletcher's *A Wife for a Month*, the death of the lovers not only seems inevitable, but we are even led to believe that Valerio has been executed, and Evanthe is only rescued as she is about to be dragged to the gallows. The danger of death is always in the foreground, disturbing any simply comic tone.

Even before the establishment of the partnership which was to produce some of the most characteristic of Jacobean tragicomedies, Francis Beaumont and John Fletcher had already, separately, tried to define their apprehension of the mixed nature of their work. Beaumont's *The Woman Hater* (1606) presents a romantic plot of love and suspicion which is disturbed not only by the pathological misogyny of Gondarino the woman hater, but also by the grotesquely comic sub-plot in which the complications of the love-quest are precisely parodied in Lazarillo's hunt for a rare gastronomic titbit. In the prologue Beaumont introduces the play as a conscious exercise in the mixture of genres: 'I dare not call it Comedy or Tragedy; 'tis perfectly neither: A Play it is, which was meant to make you laugh' (X, p. 71). Fletcher, of course, expanded this in the preface to *The Faithful Shepherdess* as he defined pastoral tragicomedy. Like Marston's plays, these early Beaumont and Fletcher tragicomedies were all written for the children's theatres. At this early stage in its development Jacobean tragicomedy seems to belong quite specifically to the private theatres and especially to the child actors with their special gift for burlesque and ironic deflation. One of Beaumont and Fletcher's greatest innovations was to introduce formally tragicomic plays, like *A King and No King* (1611), to the audiences of the public theatres.

Beaumont and Fletcher were not the first to write tragicomedy of averted danger, but it would be unwise to underestimate the impact of their unique form. It is innovatory in a number of ways. Behind the green world of romance lies a wordly wisdom without illusions. The schematic, highly patterned play *The Faithful Shepherdess* draws on *A Midsummer Night's Dream* in language and in the depiction of the pastoral world, but it covers an even wider spectrum of sexual attitudes, from celibacy to promiscuity, and the whole operates as a tissue of extreme opposites. In its sexual openness and its exploration of a variety of sexual situations the play is really closer to Dryden and Davenant's rebuilding of *The Tempest* than to *A Midsummer Night's Dream*. I have already mentioned Beaumont and Fletcher's use of some of the old archetypes of romance, girls disguised as boys, for example. These, though, can also be inverted for comic or parodic effect. The page-boy Bellario in *Philaster* is really a girl in love with her master: in *The Honest Man's Fortune* (1613), however, the faithful page, although it is frequently suggested that he is such a lovesick girl, turns out to be really only a faithful page. Again the conventional motif is parodied in a play like *The Loyal Subject* (1618), where the boy Young Archas is disguised as a girl.

As well as using or modifying the old romantic images, Beaumont and Fletcher also introduced some new ones. One is the use of a strange law which produces the agonising dilemmas of the play: Shakespeare had of course already investigated the possibilities of this in *Measure for Measure*. In *The Loyal Subject*, for instance, the law makes ingratitude a capital crime, and this law leads both to the danger of tragedy and to the happy ending. *The Queen of Corinth* turns on a law according to which a raped woman may decide whether her rapist should be executed or should be compelled to marry her. What then would happen if a man raped two women, one of whom wanted to marry him, while the other wanted his death? This image of the unlikely law was to be influential, shaping later plays like *The Old Law* (1618) and *The Partial Law* (1625). Like writers of science fiction, Beaumont and Fletcher develop a hypothesis about an alternative society and examine how its peculiarities might affect the lives of the people who inhabit it.

Perhaps a more important new image for tragicomedy is that of 'unusual wedding-night encounters'.[5] Fletcher takes drama into the bedroom. The plays have an explicit sexuality: rape (*The Queen of Corinth*) and incest (*A King and No King*), impotence (*A Wife for a Month*) and sexual disease (*The Humorous Lieutenant*), promiscuity (*The Faithful Shepherdess*), *droit de seigneur* (*The Custom of the Country*), lust and sexually motivated violence, are characteristic themes. The darker and more disturbing treatment of these themes tends to be associated especially with the later Fletcher and with his later collaborator Massinger. *A Wife for a Month* (1624), written by Fletcher alone, is particularly vivid in its use of painful sexual situations. The wicked usurper compels Valerio to marry Evanthe, whom he loves, and to submit to execution after a month. The two marry and look forward at least to a month of bliss. The usurper, though, then complicates his condition: if Valerio consummates the marriage, Evanthe will immediately be executed. In their bedroom Evanthe, who knows nothing of this latest cruelty, prepares to go to bed, making innocently bawdy advances to her husband. Valerio makes excuses and finally, agonised, pretends he is impotent. The tragicomic situaton allows a rich series of antitheses, explicit sexuality and Platonic idealism, absolutes of love and honour and scepticism about them. The plays depend on a pattern of mixed emotions, joy and sorrow, detachment and involvement, and of clashing tones and images. The iconography of tragicomedy also depends on extreme antitheses: just before its happy ending, for instance, *The Queen of Corinth* stages a powerful contrast as a colourful wedding procession with bride and priest is confronted with the black-clad executioner.

As well as its introduction of new images and a structure of extreme contrasts, Fletcherian tragicomedy is perhaps most notable for its use of surprise in the final moments which, like the dénouement of a detective story, throws into new focus the whole structure of events in the play. Marston's plays by contrast underestimate the importance of surprise. We know from the very first act of *The Malcontent* that Malevole is really the disguised duke Altofront and we learn also as the action progresses that neither Ferneze nor Pietro is really dead. The climax is surprising to the defeated Mendoza but the audience shares the superior understanding of the author and the hero. Beaumont and Fletcher on the whole make a different use of the audience. *A King and No King* presents a highly-charged plot about the temptation to commit incest. Arbaces, after struggling with his sinful passion, finally decides to rape his sister and to kill himself. The scene seems about to end as a 'tragedy' (V.4.11). Suddenly, though, the whole picture changes. It is revealed that Arbaces and Panthea are not in fact related and they can marry. The most extreme possible emotional tones collide. The audience, who are in Marston's plays as knowledgeable as the author, are here as bewildered and mistaken as the suffering people of the play. The audience has become a dramatic character.

Fletcherian tragicomedy, then, is characterised by its wide variety of tones, its structure of extreme antitheses, its avoidance of death and its abrupt change in focus by a final surprise. The plays show a disturbing world of shifting facts. Nothing seems certain: page-boys turn out to be girls, lovers turn out to be brother and sister, or brother and sister not to be related, people thought to be dead reappear alive, and so on. Metaphor turns into literal truth and literal truth into metaphor. In *The Custom of the Country*, for instance, the virtuous Zenocia is forced to submit to the lustful Count Clodio as he tries to claim *droit 'de seigneur*. She, however, stages a parody of a marriage masque in which she appears as the virgin Diana. In a tragicomic double-take this perfectly conventional metaphor becomes a literal form of militant chastity, as Zenocia turns her arrows on the Count and manages to escape with her husband.

The world of these Beaumont and Fletcher tragicomedies is a shifting and uncertain one, and characters change abruptly too: a loving man becomes insanely jealous, or a villain reforms. Consciously unreal events are filled with plausible and disquieting emotion. Even cause and effect are dislocated. In *A Wife for a Month* Valerio who seems to be dead returns alive, and at one point the virtuous Evanthe briefly pretends to be vicious. A powerful image for this uncertainty and for the equivocal relationship between cause and effect is provided when the wicked usurper gives a poisonous potion to the rightful king, who is suffering from a wasting disease. The potion, however, ironically has the reverse effect and actually cures the king. Even our assumptions about cause and effect are dubious in this dangerous world of shifting characters and situations. Clashing tones, the dislocation of cause and effect, and the shifting background all help to create the 'middle mood'[6] of Jacobean tragicomedy.

On the surface Fletcher's romantic tragicomedy sounds very different from Marston's critical, astringent and satirical form. Jacobean and Restoration writers and critics were quite sure that Beaumont and Fletcher were among the greatest authors, often ranking them with Shakespeare and Jonson. However in the nineteenth and twentieth century it has been most usual for critics to regard them as complacent decadents pandering to the prejudices of their audiences, cheerfully immoral and implausibly moralistic by turns, writers who refused to face the uncomfortable implications of the situations they created. However in the last forty years it has been possible to see that Beaumont and Fletcher do have serious moral and political concerns,[7] and to recognise the superb theatrical effectiveness of some of the best plays. It has even been possible to discern a kind of realism in the way in which distinctions of genre are minimised and in which characters are 'deflected deliberately in the direction of the small, the mean, the average'.[8] Fletcher's tragicomic characters are not unrealistically coherent and unchanging: they are inconsistent and protean in the way other people really seem to us to be, or even as we experience ourselves.[9] This discontinuous system of characterisation suggests the point where conventional methods of characterisation break down and become simplified and falsifying.

Most Jacobean playwrights, influenced by the popularity of Fletcher's tragicomedy, tried their hand at the new form. Even Shakespeare's *The Winter's Tale* (1610) is an exercise in a Fletcherian use of surprise. It is suddenly revealed at the end of the fifth act that Hermione is not dead, as her husband and the audience have believed, but has lived in retirement for sixteen years. This is the only play where Shakespeare keeps back so crucial a piece of information from the audience. In *Much Ado about Nothing* and in *All's Well that Ends Well* we always know that Hero and Helena are still alive, and we share the omniscient view of the dramatist. In *The Winter's Tale* Shakespeare experiments with a different relationship of audience and plot. We are included in Leontes' joy because Shakespeare depicts delighted surprise by making us feel it. The emotions of the audience, as they do in a Fletcherian tragicomedy, mirror and help to create those of the fictional characters.

I have already suggested that from the 1560s to the 1590s tragical comedy seemed most aware of its affinities with tragedy, but that in the hands of Beaumont and Fletcher tragicomedy became, at least structurally, closer to comedy. From 1608 to 1642 tragicomedy for the most part followed Fletcher: the tragicomedies of Middleton, Shirley and Brome, for instance, are very much in the Fletcherian mould. These plays use the Fletcherian system of antithesis, surprise and danger averted, but on the whole they lack the incisive wit of Fletcher's tragicomedies and their criticism as well as exploitation of rhetoric and convention. The most interesting tragicomedies of the period attempt not to imitate Fletcher but to find new ways of expressing tragicomic discords and double visions.

In the work of Massinger and of Ford the boundaries of the genres blur and in the case of Ford generic labels become almost meaningless. Massinger brings a new sombreness and sourness to his tragicomic conclusions, deliberately leaving loose ends or adding disturbing reservations about a happy ending. *The Maid of Honour* (1621) is perhaps Massinger's most successful attempt to synthesise the Fletcherian tragicomic pattern with his own rigorous Christian scepticism about the Fletcherian absolutes of love and honour. For its first four acts, the play seems to turn on the passionate Bertoldo's choice between two women: is he to marry the virtuous Camiola, who saves his life, whom he had loved and whom he has promised to marry, or the Duchess Aurelia with whom, suddenly and irrationally, he falls in love? However the final scene with its characteristic shift of focus reveals that this is not after all the fundamental issue. Bertoldo's problem is not choosing between two women, or even making the choice between love and honour: it is rather his conflict between his attachment to the world and his monastic vows as a Knight of Malta, which he was on the point of breaking. The play sets up and rejects the Fletcherian absolutes of love and honour to discover a religious absolute behind them. Comedy conventionally ends in marriage, but Massinger's play ironically inverts this as Camiola makes a monastic, not a worldly, 'marriage' (V.2.267) by becoming a nun. The happy ending is discordant and tentative. Cutting across the comic conventions are ominous suggestions of tragedy: Camiola has become 'dead to the world' (V.2.273) and has taken her 'last farewell' (V.2.281) of her friends. Massinger uses the images of Fletcherian tragicomedy, misunderstanding, reconciliation and marriage, but he interprets them in an unconventional way in which tragedy and comedy clash disturbingly.

Ford's plays, with their stress on pathos and silent suffering and their strange dream-like quality, also blur the dividing lines between the genres. His tragicomedies use the Fletcherian structure of clashing tones and averted danger, but they tone down and blur the extreme antitheses of Fletcher's plays. The danger which is averted is rarely the danger of death, but most characteristically danger to a woman's reputation, as in *The Lady's Trial* (1638) and *The Fancies Chaste and Noble* (1635). Ford's tragicomic surprises, too, tend to be less unexpected than in Fletcher's plays. The very title of *The Fancies Chaste and Noble* alerts us to the fact that the girls are innocent. Again in *The Lover's Melancholy* (1628) the fact that the page Parthenophil is really a girl in disguise is an open secret for much of the play, a secret which is inverted and parodied in the sub-plot, in which the lecherous Cuculus is attended by a page-boy dressed as a woman. The plays have a subdued, muted, tentative quality, and the sharp plot-lines of Fletcherian tragicomedy are blurred by the elegiac tone, the importance of pathos, and the ironic multiplication of parallel or contrasting incidents. *The Fancies* as well as *The Lover's Melancholy* has a crude sub-plot which inverts the images and values of the main plot. In play after play we are distanced from the main action by commentary in the form of debate, masque and song. Moreover the main plot tends to be resolved well before the end of the play, and this also contributes to the muted effect. In *The Lover's Melancholy* the main plot is completed by the end of Act Four, when Palador is reunited with Eroclea, and in *The Fancies* the main plot is more or less completed in the penultimate scene. Ford seems to need a scene, or even a whole act, to move the audience back from the enacted fiction to real life. In the last scene of *The Fancies*, the discovery of the truth leads to reconciliation, and danger is replaced by a subdued joy tinged with pathos: 'The Bower of Fancies is quite withered' (p. 213). Also in this last scene, the main plot is paraphrased and parodied in a masque which describes love and its effects. In Ford's tragicomedies the single disorientating surprise is replaced by muted emotions, a stress on pathos, and a tissue of double-images.

Ford and Massinger minimise the distinction between the genres. Thomas Heywood was interested in many forms of the mixed play, writing Fletcherian plays like *The Royal King and the Loyal Subject,* patriotic-romantic extravaganza like *The Fair Maid of the West,* history and myth interspersed with clowning, like the *Ages* plays. His most startling divergence from Fletcherian practice, though, is in some plays in which tragicomedy is firmly based on tragedy, and especially *The English Traveller* and *The Rape of Lucrece. The English Traveller* (1625) is described as a 'tragicomedy' in the epistle to the reader, and as 'a strange play' in the prologue.[10] It is a 'strange play' partly because it contains none of the elaborate visual effects we might expect:

> No combat, marriage, not so much today
> As song, dance, masque, to bombast out a play.   (p. 155)

It provides simply 'bare lines' (p. 155). It is a strange play in more than its bareness, however. The plot is potentially tragic, but it is parodied and undercut by a farcical sub-plot as well as by its own equivocal nature. In the main plot Young Geraldine falls in love with the young wife of Old Wincott, a good old man who is a trusting friend of Geraldine. Geraldine and Mrs Wincott vow to marry after the death of her husband, but to remain chaste during his lifetime. Geraldine's false friend Delavil, however, seduces the weak Mrs Wincott, and when Geraldine discovers this the woman dies of shame and a broken heart. The play is deliberately untidy and anticlimactic, and potential tragedy is undercut by its insistence upon mixed feelings. As the play ends a 'feast' has been turned 'into a funeral' (p. 248). Young Geraldine and Wincott are to 'feast, and after mourn . . ./wear blacks without, but other thoughts within' (p. 248). This play, like *The Maid of Honour*, ends with the conventional image of marriage which is given an unconventional interpretation, the 'marriage of . . . love' (p. 248) between Old Wincott and Young Geraldine. Heywood's unFletcherian form includes farce and death but undermines both the tragic absolutes and the conventions of comedy.

The Rape of Lucrece (1607) also establishes a tragic structure but undermines it. Heywood might also have called this a 'strange play'. It falls into two quite distinct parts. The first half is crammed with clowns and gentlemen wearing an antic disposition, with songs, especially comic or outrageously bawdy songs, with jokes, puns and satirical commentary, with laughter and the language of comedy. In a profoundly disordered society the genres too are disordered. With the suicide of Lucrece the whole quality of the play changes. There are no more jokes, songs or laughter: the Roman nobles cast off the protective colouring of comedy and destroy the Tarquins. However *The Rape of Lucrece* establishes a tragicomic double vision not only in the clear dichotomy between the play's two parts: the presentation of the rape itself is profoundly ambiguous. Lucrece is a type of virtue, the ideal wife and woman, and in isolation the rape has a certain stylised pathos. Nonetheless it is surrounded on all sides by irreverent comedy and obscenity. After the rape Valerius, a friend of Collatine and Lucrece, joins the Clown to sing startlingly obscene songs about her. The bawdy catch about the rape with its chorus of laughter especially complicates our attitude to the central incident and undermines its tragic potential:

> Did he take fair Lucrece by the toe, man?
> Toe, man?
> Ay, man.
> Ha ha ha ha ha man!
> And further did he strive to go, man?
> Go, man?
> Ay, man.
> Ha ha ha ha, man, fa derry derry down, ha fa derry dino!
>
> (p. 401)

From the earliest Renaissance to the Restoration period, tragicomic dramatists more or less grudgingly defended their hybrid form by insisting that they were simply giving their audiences what they wanted. Cinthio, he tells us, would have preferred to call his serious plays with happy endings tragedies: he had Aristotelian precedent for this. However he was afraid his audience would be daunted by the seriousness of this term and he therefore used the label 'tragicomedy'.[11] Again in *The White Devil* The Duke of Florence suggests that a 'tragedy' must contain 'idle mirth' so that it might 'pass' with audiences (IV.1.119–20).

Why was this so? Some of the reasons are obvious. Tragicomedy can allow the audience to experience an enormous emotional range within its narrow confines and it completes its emotional seesaw with a happy ending. The use of surprise and suspense has also proved successful in the popular culture of all ages. As Webster pointed out, the mixture of modes seems always to have appealed to popular audiences: tragicomic forms are 'founded psychologically on the popular audience's ability to shift rapidly its modes of attention',[12] and its liking for doing so.

But, as I have suggested, Jacobean tragicomedy was not as simple as that. Behind the clear-cut structure of sharp contrasts, surprise and suspense, lurks a teasing double-vision, a critical ability to see events simultaneously in very different ways. The tragicomic double-vision may sometimes depend on a multiple plot structure, despite Guarini's stricture that the true tragicomic plot is mixed rather than double. In Marston's *The Dutch Courtesan* the sub-plot, in which the knavish Cocledemoy cheats the hypocritical Puritan Mulligrub, is a distorting mirror of the main plot, in which the worldly-wise Frevil tricks and educates Malheureux, the man of a 'professed abstinence' (I.2.109–10), who has betrayed his own high ideals by falling in love with the courtesan. Malheureux's convincing pain and passion have an almost tragic intensity, but both are undermined by the precise comparisons made with the grasping and ridiculous Mulligrub. The play operates as a tissue of opposites: the two plots cast ironic light upon each other and their characters are compared and contrasted.

The characteristic tragicomic double-vision, though, does not need a multiple plot structure: one of Fletcher's achievements is to bring the romantic and the anti-romantic into close juxtaposition within the same plot. We expect Marston to undermine what he seems to praise. Frevil in *The Dutch Courtesan* is such a mixed character, a hero whose motives are none the less rather shabby, as he himself is the first to admit:

> But is this virtue in me? No, not pure;
> Nothing extremely best with us endures.   (IV.2.39–40)

However even Fletcher's apparently more romantic form also adopts this method of ironic deflation. *Philaster* is typical of the Fletcherian use of an ironic double-vision. The play as usual is built on a tissue of opposites, and we are constantly forced to make comparisons.

Philaster the true heir is contrasted with the usurping king and with the lecherous prince Pharamond, and the virtuous Arethusa is contrasted with the grotesque wanton Megra and with the more equivocal Bellario, a woman who follows Philaster in male disguise. More important, however, are the ambiguities centred on the character of Philaster himself. On the surface he seems a perfect romantic figure, a prince robbed of his inheritance but loved by the people because of his virtue, the 'bravery of his mind' (I, p. 76),[13] and his courage: indeed 'He is the worthiest the true name of man / This day' (p. 81). As the play goes on, though, one is forced increasingly to question this view. Especially in the scenes of the hunt, which provides a rather sinister image for the love-relationship, Philaster appears a far more dubious character than this chorus of praise would suggest. His passionate unreasonableness and his violence appear slightly ludicrous when confronted with a less extreme view of life. As Philaster, goaded by false reports of her infidelity, is about to kill the woman he loves, he is interrupted by a Country Fellow who brings with him a less rarefied and more sympathetic code of values: 'Hold dastard, strike a Woman!' (I, p. 125). Both the rhetorical fury of Philaster and Arethusa's aggressive submissiveness are undermined, and the values of the extreme world of romance are called into question.

Similarly in *A King and No King* our view of Arbaces' tragic and heroic potential is modified by the uneasy excesses in his own nature, and by the commentary of sensible men like Mardonius. More important, the coward and boaster Bessus is a distorted and parodic version of Arbaces himself. The play opens with Mardonius and Bessus discussing the war which has just ended: Bessus' bragging (I.1.52–3) is mocked by Mardonius. Later in the same scene Mardonius also rebukes Arbaces for his boasting (I.1.119–240). Throughout the play, Bessus and Arbaces are compared in their uncritical self-esteem, faulty judgement, and rhetorical excesses. Finally both gain happiness by a verbal redefinition: Arbaces discovers that he and Panthea are not brother and sister and so can marry, and Bessus escapes a beating by a similar redefinition of identity: 'Bessus the coward wrong'd you ... And shall Bessus the valiant maintain what Bessus the coward did?' (III.2.118–21). Heroic qualities in Arbaces coexist with deflating commentary and parody. This tactic of undermining the absolute which the play has seemed to affirm is central to the sceptical vision of Fletcherian tragicomedy.

Tragicomedy, then, appeals not only by its use of surprise and the happy ending, but also by its use of alternating viewpoints and its frustration of our expectations. Another aspect of its double-vision is the use of ironic repetition so that two incidents or characters are brought into an unexpected focus and we are asked to compare apparently different events and people. This may work to deflate a serious romantic moment or to add poignancy to a comic one, and it helps to give coherence to the tragicomic structure of opposites. *The Tempest*, for instance, makes much use of repetition and comparison, especially in the final act. When Caliban looks at the reforming society at the end of the play and exclaims, 'These be brave spirits indeed!' (V.1.261), we are obviously meant to be reminded of Miranda's 'Oh brave new world!' (V.1.183). Even the 'thing of darkness' (V.1.275) is included, however precariously, in the comic ending, just as is the innocent Miranda. In Marston's *The Dutch Courtesan* tragicomic discords operate through the double plot structure, but are also reinforced by ironic repetition. The tragic possibilities inherent in the situation of Malheureux especially are undercut by ironic repetition of words and incidents. As Frevil prepares to visit the courtesan, Malheureux ends the scene tidily with a sententious couplet:

> Well, I'll go to make her loathe the shame she's in.
> The sight of vice augments the hate of sin.   (I.1.152–3)

Frevil immediately punctures this: 'The sight of vice augments the hate of sin! / Very fine, perdy!' (I.1.154–5). Later when Malheureux falls in love with the Courtesan Frevil again ironically repeats his expressions of pain: 'Oh, that to love should be or shame or sin!' (I.2.154). Extremely different tones clash: Malheureux's pain becomes simply Frevil's 'Laughter eternal!' (I.2.137).

Tragicomedy, then, seems to deserve a treatment more serious than the dismissal it has sometimes received. It offers variety and surprise. It sets up ideals but questions them. It modifies our reactions to events and characters by multiplication and ironic antithesis and repetition. I have left until last, though, perhaps the two most interesting facets of tragicomedy's critical nature. First, and I shall reserve this for my next chapter, tragicomedy establishes a particularly rich and close relationship between audience and play. Secondly, tragicomedy criticises as well as exploits its own peculiar rhetoric.

An important way in which the dramatist can draw the attention of his audience to the play as artefact is by describing the nature and function of its own dramatic language. Shakespeare in *Love's Labour's Lost* and Jonson in *The Poetaster* are explicitly interested in kinds of language and the point where language fails. This simultaneous use and criticism of rhetoric is an important part of the effect of the tragicomedy of Marston, Beaumont and Fletcher, and their successors. Marston has often been, in his own day and since, ridiculed for his passionate and flamboyant, and sometimes grotesque and cacophanous, language, but he was himself the first to criticise it. In his plays, for instance, highly-charged emotional language is almost always undercut and ridiculed, especially by the use of play images. Malevole urges the despairing Pietro 'do not rand, do not turn player' (*The Malcontent* IV.4.5), and in *What You Will* Quadratus mocks the rhetoric of the love-sick Iacomo: 'He speaks like a player, hah! poetical!' (II, p. 238).

Samuel Schoenbaum has accused Marston's work of being 'inarticulate . . . incoherent . . . hysterical'.[14] However it seems to me that he is rather a writer who is interested in the inarticulate and the incoherent as other ways in which men prove themselves inadequate for the rôles they are called upon to play, a linguistic parallel for Malheureux's inability to live up to his own strict moral code. In play after play Marston sees the breakdown of language as a symptom of the breakdown of society, and both are also mirrored in the breakdown of simple distinctions of genre. This breakdown of language appears in its most comic form in *What You Will*, where Albano's stutter at moments of stress, and Francisco's mimicry of it, provide a ludicrous example of the failure of language and man's failure to live up to his image of his own nobility. In other plays the broken English of Franceschina or John fo de King, Piero's stutter, Antonio's or Balurdo's inability to finish similes, or Granuffo's silence, all suggest that men are essentially incoherent and that words, the very medium of the plays, may be untrustworthy.

'Babel' is one of Marston's favourite images for this tragicomic undermining of language, and it is punningly associated with 'Babylon', the sinful city, so that vice and incoherence seem two closely connected failures of society. *The Malcontent* opens with 'the vilest out-of-tune music' (I.1. initial SD), the audible sign that the play is 'building Babylon' (I.1.2), presenting a court where sin rules and where language appears distorted into grotesque and extreme forms. Malevole–Altofront controls the relationship between his two identities as malcontent and as rightful duke by using two different kinds of language, and to switch from one personality to another he simply 'shifteth his speech' (I.4.43 SD).

The two parts of the mixed *Antonio and Mellida* most clearly investigate the point where language collapses, and the failure of language under pressure undermines some of the play's most apparently tragic moments. Speeches are repeatedly broken off, sentences left unfinished, as characters thrash about for a suitable word or simile. The fool Balurdo regularly fails to complete his sentences: 'Now would I be that toy, to put you in the head kindly to conceit my – my – my – pray you give m'an epithet for love' (*A&M* II.1.220–2). However the inability to use language significantly is by no means confined to the comic characters. The virtuous Feliche accuses the wicked Piero of 'this Babel pride', which the tyrant answers and proves by replying in Latin with a Senecan tag (*A&M* I.1.59). Later Piero is reduced to complete incoherence by the disappearance of his daughter: 'I know not who – who – who – what I do – do – do – nor who – who – where I am . . .' (*A&M* II.2.175–7). Even the tragic potential of the young lovers is disturbed by their failure to use language successfully. Antonio breaks off, leaving a sentence unfinished, to take part in a love-dialogue with Mellida in Italian: a page who listens suggests that 'confusion of Babel is fall'n upon these lovers' (*A&M* IV.1.219). Elsewhere language simply fails Antonio: 'she comes like – O no simile / Is precious choice enough' (I.1.151–3), 'And thou and I will live – / Let's think like what – and thou and I will live / Like unmatched mirrors of calamity' (II.1.295–7). At the end of the two plays, in the ultimate statement of the failure of language, the assassins tear out Piero's tongue: 'we'll spoil your oratory' (*AR* V.5.33).

Beaumont and Fletcher are usually less flamboyant in their discussion of the failure of language, but it is still very frequently present as a theme. Many critics have recognised that the two dramatists make much use of consciously rhetorical language, even deriving plots from that handbook for orators the *Contraversiae* of Seneca the Elder. Muriel Bradbrook has written that in the Beaumont and Fletcher plays 'there is no verbal framework of any kind', and she notes 'the decay of the linguistic patterns' of the earlier drama in these plays.[15] It is certainly true that these plays do not develop a 'verbal framework' through the use of iterative imagery in the Shakespearean or Websterian manner, but the tragicomedies do approach a 'verbal framework' by their sceptical criticism of the rhetorical devices which they use. The Beaumont and Fletcher plays seem acutely aware of the collapse of the social structures of the sixteenth century, and also of the sixteenth century faith in language. In their plays passionate and highly-coloured speeches are repeatedly undercut, sometimes by our awareness of their fictional basis, sometimes by ironic positioning, sometimes by direct criticism. In *Philaster*, for instance, the Country Fellow who disturbs the high romantic world of the fourth act also undermines the rhetoric of love and death: 'I know not your Rhetoric, but I can lay it on you if you touch the woman' (I, p. 125). The passionate and rarefied rhetoric of Philaster and Arethusa is immediately discredited.

In two of Fletcher's independent tragicomedies the whole situation of pain and danger is directly created by the breakdown of the traditional rhetoric or by the failure of some character to understand it. In *The Mad Lover* the Princess whimsically pretends to take literally the love-sick Memnon's wish to give her his 'truly loving heart' (III, p. 15), and Memnon is himself unable to distinguish whether she is in earnest or in jest. In *A Wife for a Month* the wicked usurper insists on giving a literal interpretation to the love-rhetoric of Valerio's poem to Evanthe:

> To be your own but one poor Month, I'd give
> My Youth, my Fortune, and then leave to live.   (V, p. 11)

The conventional rhetoric of love is finally untrustworthy. People misunderstand the metaphors of others or mistake literal statements for metaphorical ones. Language hinders real communication as much as it helps: by distorting what we mean it creates action as well as expressing it.

Perhaps *A King and No King* particularly shows the way that language creates and distorts action. The play constantly stresses the power, but also the impotence, of words. Tigranes' 'name' (I.2.98) is enough to terrify Arbaces' people. Sometimes, however, language fails, so that the king's 'words move nothing' (I.1.306). This ambiguity runs very deep into the fabric of the play. The whole passion and pain of the action depends on the two flimsy words 'brother' and 'sister', which are 'mere sounds' (IV.4.113), 'merely voice' (IV.4.126), and yet can create impassible barriers. The play's critical treatment of language is clearest in the treatment of 'brother' and 'sister', and in ambiguities about 'king' and 'queen', but it is also tellingly demonstrated in a comic incident. When Arbaces returns victorious from the wars he makes a typical self-glorifying speech about his winning of 'peace'. The listening people misunderstand and imagine he has brought home 'peas for all our money' (II.2.149–50). Arbaces' view of himself as a conquering hero is grotesquely reduced to the image of a grocer bringing his vegetables to market. This deflating pun undermines not only Arbaces' secure sense of his own worth, but also our uncritical faith in his ability to use words. In a sense it seems that in *A King and No King* the basic concerns are not personal, political or moral but semantic: even the title is a semantic puzzle.

Tragicomedy, then, provides not just arresting plots of extreme opposites and a wide emotional range: at its best it is also critical of its own conventions and especially of its own rhetoric. This theme of the deceptive nature of language and of the difficulty of distinguishing literal from metaphorical language is an important one in Jacobean tragicomedy, pioneered by Marston and by Beaumont and Fletcher, and explored particularly closely by John Webster: *The Devil's Law-case* is, among other things, an analysis of the failure of language.

3

'Spectators sate part': the audience and the tragicomic ending

It is a commonplace of Elizabethan drama that the step from audience to actor could be a very narrow one indeed. The murderous masque which ends so many Jacobean tragedies, and the marriage-masque of comedy in which a union is made or celebrated, both depend on an inversion by which actor can suddenly become spectator or spectator actor. Richard Brome's sparkling 'comedy about the art of comedy' *The Antipodes* (1638)[1] stages a grotesque play within the play in which all values are inverted as psychiatric therapy for a number of disturbed or maladjusted characters. As the Doctor points out, they are to be cured by involving themselves in the fictional action, 'not alone / Spectators, but ... actors' (II.1.42–43). The drama of the period is full of similar examples where the clear dividing line between performer and spectator is blurred. The very structure of the Elizabethan playhouse encouraged this: in public or private theatres members of the audience might sit on the stage, surrounded by the play, 'on the very rushes where the Comedy is to dance, yea and under the State of Cambyses himself'.[2] It is small wonder that the dramatists seem to have been especially interested in analysing the relationship of audience and play, or in presenting images of this changing relationship, or in using the audience as a dramatic character.

Part of the attraction of tragicomedy may well have been the especially clear and direct way in which the genre uses, mirrors, involves and defers to its audience. The Fletcherian use of surprise suddenly introduces a new kind of relationship between audience and play. Marston's mixed plays often present an audience watching a drama. This is not unique to tragicomedy: Revenge and the ghost of Andrea watch *The Spanish Tragedy*, and this larger pattern is reflected in little as the court watches Hieronimo's entertainment of the three knights, and later the play of Soliman and Perseda. Still, no

40

dramatist makes such constant use of the device as Marston. *Histriomastix* and *The Malcontent* stage included plays or masques, *The Malcontent, What You Will, Jack Drum's Entertainment* and *Antonio and Mellida* begin with inductions featuring actors, members of the audience and other workers in the playhouse. Sometimes these inductions reflect the real ambivalence of the author's attitude towards his audience. *Jack Drum's Entertainment* begins with the Tireman's report that the author is trying to prevent the performance, 'and with violence keeps the boys from coming on the stage' (III, p. 179). This is explained as a demonstration of the author's diffidence about the unworthiness of the play for its 'generous' spectators, but even this gracious compliment does not quite destroy the violence of this initial gesture of the author against actors and audience. In *What You Will* actors playing three members of the audience 'sit a good while on the stage' (II, p. 231) before the play begins. They insult actors, author and play, 'a slight toy, lightly composed, too swiftly finished, ill plotted, worse written, I fear me worst acted' (II, p. 233), raising objections to the play before members of the real audience can do so. Marston directs the audience's responses to the mixed play by mixed and tentative descriptions of genre, and by elaborate prologues and inductions which reflect the audience themselves.

After their first tragicomedies for the children's theatres, Beaumont and Fletcher do not present their audience so directly with images of themselves. With the exception of *Four Plays in One*, Fletcher did not show actors playing members of an audience in any of his works, although his collaborators Beaumont and Massinger certainly did so. Beaumont's *The Knight of the Burning Pestle* (1607) is an exercise in and parody of the direct Marstonian presentation of the audience, and Massinger's *The Roman Actor* (1626) presents a series of included plays which mirror the audience and in which fiction and reality shift bewilderingly. Even Fletcher's one direct staging of the audience in *Four Plays in One* presents not the audience of the commercial theatres at all, but rather the exclusive audience of the court, and the play is very little interested in examining the rôle of the audience.

However, although Beaumont and Fletcher rarely depict their audience directly, from the date of the 1646 Folio they were praised for the way in which the audience is assigned a specific rôle in their plays. T. Palmer of Christ Church, Oxford, in his inaugural verses to the Folio writes of this power of engaging the audience:

Like Scenes, we shifted Passions, and that so,
Who only came to see, turn'd Actors too.   (I, p. xlviii)

The plays do not present actors playing members of the audience: it is rather that the rôles of audience and actors merge. Joseph Mayne also says as much in his commendatory verses: 'Spectators sate part in your Tragedies' (I, p. xxxvi). The audience has the status of a dramatic character, involved in the emotional patterning, as puzzled or ill-informed as the people of the play. Because Beaumont and Fletcher moved easily between the public and private theatres they were not restricted to one set of dramatic definitions. They synthesised the close and direct audience–play relationship and the concern for mixed genres which we associate with the children's theatres with the public theatre's avoidance of the loose satirical structure of plays like Marston's and its stress on involvement as well as detachment.

This special relationship with the audience in tragicomedy is often clearest at the ending of the play, where the dramatist must help his audience to make a complex readjustment from their absorption in the enacted fiction to their return to real life. In a play which uses the colliding tones and definitions of tragicomedy this clear guidance about the boundary between fiction and real life seems particularly important. The final scenes of some plays, like *Love's Labour's Lost* or *The Malcontent* or *The Devil's Law-case* or *The Lover's Melancholy* or *A Jovial Crew*, stage an included play, masque or pageant which reveals on a smaller scale the line between fiction and real life. The ending of this included play prepares for the ending of the parent play and reminds us of its fictional nature. Even if a formal play within the play is not staged, the final scene may be rich in play imagery or in play equivalents: the confrontation and the progressive shedding of disguise in the last scene of *Measure for Measure*, or the slow and laborious explication of fictions in the last scene of *All's Well that Ends Well*, form play-equivalents. Some plays even prepare us for their ending by actually presenting imagery of the fictional ending. The hero of Ben Jonson's *The New Inn* quotes Donne in order to compare his emotional disorientation to 'a court removing, or an ended play' (IV.4.252).[3] As early as Act Four of *The Tempest* Prospero stages the Masque of Goddesses which dissolves prematurely as the cares of real life impinge upon it, and through it Prospero warns us about the coming dissolution of the play itself, and also about the differences, and the similarities, between real life and the enacted fiction:

The solemn temples, the great globe itself,
Yea, all which it inherit, shall dissolve,
And, like this insubstantial pageant faded,
Leave not a rack behind.   (IV.1.153–6)

Here even the theatrical pun in 'globe' warns us that we are watching a play, and that the theatrical fiction, like the world which it mirrors, is poignantly precarious.

Some plays finally turn to the audience and lead them back to the real world by admitting even more directly the fictional nature of the events in which we have so recently been absorbed. A dramatic character reveals himself as simply an actor, a highly-charged plot is seen in retrospect as only a fiction. Shakespeare seems to recognise particularly clearly the necessity for such a mediating conclusion, especially in plays which have mocked or attacked our complacent assumptions about the genres. An epilogue is used several times to return us to the real world, to reveal the actor behind a dramatic character, and to point out how at the end of the fiction the established relationship of audience and play changes. At the end of *The Tempest* Prospero moves from the magic island to the 'bare island' (Epilogue 8) of the stage. At the end of *All's Well that Ends Well* the actor playing the King of France steps out of his part to speak the epilogue. He announces that he is no longer a king but 'a beggar' (1), an actor touting for applause, a member of a profession classed with rogues and vagabonds. He turns to the audience, making the conventional request for applause and the conventional statement of the power of the audience to bring the play to its happy ending. At the same time he suggests that as the play ends, the positions of audience and performers are reversed: 'Ours be your patience then and yours our parts' (Epilogue 5). The actors watch passively as the audience take over the active rôle and applaud, and the audience return from the ending fiction to resume their places as actors in their own lives.

Some of Shakespeare's tragicomic endings mediate for the audience between the play and the world by staging an included play in the last scene, or by a formal epilogue in which a character, major or minor, steps out of his fictional rôle to guide the audience out of the fiction. Beaumont and Fletcher rarely use either of these images of ending directly. More characteristically, they fill final scenes with play-images, or even more obliquely they remind us of the fictional nature of what we are watching by exploring some theatrical problems like the significant use of language. The mediating process tends to be buried deeper in the plot than in many Marstonian or Shakespearean tragicomic endings. *A King and No King* has neither epilogue nor included play, but the long narrative in the final scene in which the truth about Arbaces' birth is revealed has a similar function as a narrative within the narrative: in some early versions this is even given in prose to section it off more clearly from the blank verse of the surrounding play.[4] It is as if the dramatic mode of the play has been momentarily suspended to be replaced by a narrative mode, as its fictions are replaced by a new understanding of the truth. Arbaces is not king by birth, and therefore Panthea is not his sister. This movement from fiction to truth predicts, like a play within the play, the similar movement from fiction as the play itself ends. Like the epilogue, this use of narrative also marks a change in the relationship of audience and play. Throughout the play Arbaces has fought and agonised and ranted: now he simply listens, mirroring our faculty as audience, so that again we are watching ourselves watching, and again the audience is drawn into the centre of the play. So intense is the involvement of the audience in the action that we need a relatively flat, distancing passage to help us to make the readjustment between this intense involvement and our return to the real world. Sometimes, as in *A King*, this passage is incorporated into the narrative. Sometimes, as the commendatory verses to the Folio tell us, it takes the form of an epilogue outside the action:

> We could not stir away
> Until the epilogue told us 'twas a Play.[5]

In the mediating ending, then, the playwright helps the audience to adjust to the return to real life by presenting a sequence of images of play, audience and the dramatic ending, by an epilogue in which an actor sloughs off his fictional identity, or by discussion of the nature of drama. These effects are most prominent in plays of equivocal genre. In *Love's Labour's Lost* the use of the audience and the discussion of the nature of drama and the dramatic ending are richly mixed in tone. The last act includes two dramas within the drama, the Masque of Russians and the Pageant of the Nine Worthies, both of which go disconcertingly wrong for their actors. In the Masque of Russians the rôles of performers and audience are reversed as the ladies, whom the men intend to use as an audience, themselves assume disguises and take over the control of the fiction, mocking the men and tricking them into perjuring themselves again. They even deflate the love-rhetoric of the men by refusing to respond to their metaphors. Rosaline insists that men who have measured many miles must know the number of inches in one mile (V.2.188–9), Berowne asks for 'one sweet word' and is given 'honey, and milk, and sugar' (V.2.230–1). In the second enacted fiction, the Pageant of the Nine Worthies, the relationship between audience and play again collapses. The ladies watch silently and sympathetically but the men mock and disrupt the fiction. They insist that it is they, the audience, who create and control the dramatic fiction by accepting it and responding to it. It is solely by their good-will that the actors can enter the fiction and assume new identities: 'We have given thee faces' (V.2.614.)

These two complementary views of the enacted fiction examine the relationship of audience and play, alert the audience in the theatre that what they are watching is a fiction, and prepare them for the ending of the play. At the same time something else is happening: wit-skirmishes and the golden world of 'comedy' (V.2.462) are increasingly undermined by a disturbing recognition of the reality of violence and death. Katherine discloses that her sister died of love (V.2.14–15), Armado asks for respect for the dead Hector: 'The sweet war-man is dead and rotten: . . . when he breathed, he was a man' (V.2.653–5). Finally the messenger Mercade enters with the news of the death of the Princess's father. The entrance of the messenger of death into the festive setting of comedy is doubly poignant because it mirrors so precisely what is to happen when the play ends. The pageant over, the demands and fears of real life reassert themselves and the audience, arrogant in their ability to control the dramatic fiction, must face the less accommodating material of reality. So strong is this final scene's interest in its audience that Rosaline's final test of her lover even leads into a graceful compliment to the audience:

A jest's prosperity lies in the ear
Of him that hears it, never in the tongue
Of him that makes it.   (V.2.849–51)

This turning to the audience in the play's most poignant moment leads to a comparison between a conventional comic form and the convincing untidiness of the play. Jack hath not Jill. The comic patterns remain incomplete, and we are finally watching neither 'an old play' (V.2.862) nor a conventional 'comedy' (V.2.864). The play ends, not with the traditional marriages, but inconclusively. We are promised a happy ending but it lies somewhere in the uncertain future, and 'that's too long for a play' (V.2.866). The comic framework has shattered, and so has the easy and intimate relationship of audience and play. Finally actors and audience must separate, 'You that way: we this way' (V.2.918–19).

A play ending mediates for the audience between the world of the play and the workaday world, often by presenting theatrical images, by using explicity theatrical language, or by drawing our attention to its nature as artifice. *The Tempest* or *The Malcontent* use especially images of play and playwright, *Love's Labour's Lost* and *A King and No King* especially that of the audience. This mediating ending is not, of course, confined to tragicomedy and plays of equivocal genre. Comedy often uses this mediating conclusion: in the epilogue to *As You Like It* the boy actor playing Rosalind steps out of his rôle to end the play. Even *Hamlet* approaches, in a rather more subdued way, the mediating conclusion. The final scene makes much use, in a political and courtly sense, of words of whose theatrical undertones we cannot be unaware: 'prologue', 'play', 'audience', 'stage', and 'shows'.[6] Again as audience we are reminded that what we are watching is simply an enacted fiction, and we are prepared for its ending and for our return to our everyday life. Nowhere, though, is this process more important or more complex than it is in tragicomedy, where colliding tones make this process of mediation and clarification particularly necessary.

This mediating conclusion is not restricted to tragicomedy or even to drama. The necessity for the author to help reader or observer to readjust between fiction and real life at the end of the fiction must be faced by any writer of narrative. Frank Kermode has examined the nature of fictional conclusions in *The Sense of an Ending*. We have, he suggests, a 'deep need for intelligible Ends'.[7] He also quotes George Eliot's summing up of the difficulties posed to the writer by these intelligible ends: 'Conclusions are the weak point of most authors . . . Some of the fault lies in the very nature of a conclusion, which is at best a negation'.[8] The fiction has presented a model of the world, and as it ends we cannot but become aware that this model is not quite the world as we know it. The ending might thus destroy rather than complete the fictional world. Writers occasionally make studied and ironic use of this negating ending, the ending which shatters the fiction and brings us back sharply and painfully to real life. Gay in *The Beggar's Opera* and Brecht in *The Threepenny Opera* give a deliberately derisory and blatantly unconvincing happy ending to the action of crime and betrayal in order to mock their audience's love of escapist fiction. Eric Bentley's comment on happy endings seems especially relevant to plays like these: 'Happy endings are always ironical (like everything else that is happy in comedy)'.[9]

Even where they do not intend to mock their audiences like Gay or Brecht, writers have always had to face the problem that the pat ending will simply undermine the fiction which it completes. Dickens had to rewrite the ending of *Great Expectations*, and he finally left it teasingly ambiguous. Pip 'saw no shadow of another parting from' Estella.[10] Does this mean that they are to part for ever or that they are, finally, to marry? The writer of fiction must maintain the difficult balance between admitting the fictional nature of his narrative and insisting on the significance of this fiction and its relationship with real life.

The problem of 'intelligible Ends' seems most pressing in drama, which exists not only between the pages of a book but also in physical form on stage, and where the descent of the curtain, the concluding jig or curtain call, and the return home from the theatre provide such concrete images of the ending of fiction. Moreover, the fear that the ending may offer only a negation seems especially relevant to tragicomedy, where negation so often plays a significant part in dramatic endings. In *A King and No King* even the facts which we had thought to be established are negated: the play is not a 'tragedy' (V.4.11) because Arbaces and Panthea are not really brother and sister. However the ending is not only an ironic negation. The mode of the play changes from dramatic to narrative, and Arbaces becomes a representative of the audience as well as an actor. By watching Arbaces as audience, we are assigned a place in the dramatic dilemma: as the new information is heard first by Arbaces and then, more imperfectly, by the courtiers and Panthea, we are confronted by a series of images of our own rôle in the process of performance. Instead of creating an absolute dividing line between fiction and real life, the play in its final moments presents the audience with images of themselves. At his conclusion a dramatist, and especially a tragicomic dramatist, must establish a firm relationship between the ending fiction and the continuing life of the audience, here by showing actors reflecting the audience's own status as involved observers. In Frank Kermode's terms, endings are satisfactory only when they do not simply negate but also 'frankly transfigure the events in which they are immanent'.[11]

Finally I want to look at some ways in which the tragicomic ending negates or transfigures the fiction by examining in some detail the final scene of Marston's *The Malcontent* (1604). In this concluding scene a masque is staged in which the rightful duke sheds his malcontent disguise and the wicked usurper is defeated. The masque is a form which traditionally describes and heralds harmony, and *The Malcontent* moves clearly towards this comic reconciliation. The play opens with a striking image of discord, as 'the vilest out-of-tune music' (I.1.initial SD) is heard from the malcontent's chamber. It ends with the reimposition of harmony in masque and dance, and with Altofront's return to his real identity as philosopher–king.

The last scene of the play opens with the courtiers taking their places for Celso's masque. The introduction to the dramatic presentation with its satirical and critical view of the relationship of audience and play may well have inspired Webster's induction to the whole play, to which it forms a parallel. The violence of this scene, with its hysterical and strident insistence on enjoyment – 'The music! more lights, revelling, scaffolds, do you hear?' (V.4.7–8) – provides a distorted image of the audience in the theatre. The final masque, with its consciousness of fiction and its presentation of audience and actors, forms a dramatic bridge, leading the audience in the theatre out of the play and preparing them for their return from the ordered fiction to the real world.

As the masque is about to begin, the moment of uneasy festivity is further complicated by the entrance of the penitent Aurelia and by the virtuous Maria's serene acceptance of her own death. The tragic potential of this small antimasque, however, is immediately dissipated. Mercury, who 'presents the masque' (V.4.101), enters. In ordering the masque the usurper Mendoza had himself suggested its conventional motif, 'some brave spirits of the Genoan dukes ... / Led in by Mercury' (V.3.60–2). Celso's ironic masque, however, interprets this conventional iconography in a surprisingly literal manner. Mercury introduces himself as the 'god of ghosts' (V.4.91) and presents some of these 'ghosts', 'Malevole, Pietro, Ferneze and Celso in white robes, with dukes' crowns' (V.4.101 SD). Of the masquers, all but Celso are believed by the people in the play to be dead. As deposed dukes, moreover, Malevole and Pietro personate the spirits of the Genoan dukes in an unexpectedly exact way. The discovery that what had seemed to be fiction is turning into fact prepares us for the final banishment of fiction and the return to fact as the play ends.

Metaphorical and literal truth blur for a moment before they finally separate.

The masque ends as fiction explodes into the primary world of the play and the usurper Mendoza finds himself at the mercy of his enemies. The consequent discarding of disguise by the masquers is unexpectedly complex. One of the masquers, disguised as the spirit of a duke, reveals himself as the malcontent Malevole, but even the Malevole identity is merely a disguise for Altofront, the rightful duke. Mendoza is seized and insulted, but as befits a tragicomedy his life is spared. The tragicomic ending is almost complete, its reconciliation troubled hardly at all by the ejection of Mendoza and only slightly more so by Altofront's sombre and unillusioned theorising.

One final effect still remains. Altofront's sequence of disguises has been yet more complicated. The whole fictional framework collapses into 'delusions' (V.4.148) and a 'dream' (V.4.149) as Altofront casts off layer by layer the disguises he is wearing. He expounds one of the fundamental problems of theatrical experience, the nature of dramatic illusion. 'Th'inconstant people' (V.4.174) are taken in by 'outward shows' (V.4.174), by those of actors no less than by those of kings. Suddenly the highly-charged plot of integrity and pretence has collapsed to leave only a few men standing aimlessly on a stage. The discarding of disguise in this fictional plot is a powerful image for the play's own abandonment of fiction. Altofront, who has already shed the fictional identities of masquer and malcontent, now sheds that last fictional identity and is left simply as Richard Burbage, an actor: 'The rest of idle actors idly part' (V.4.194).

The final scenes of tragicomic plays like *The Malcontent* and *A King and No King* accept that the dramatic ending is necessarily a negation, *The Malcontent* by shedding fiction altogether and revealing the participants as simply actors, *A King and No King* by overturning so violently our assumptions about the play, even about its dividing line between actors and audience. However both endings also give more than simple negation. In Kermode's words they 'transfigure' their material by placing the fictional events in a new context and by leading the audience out of the play and back into the workaday world. In my succeeding chapters I shall be looking at the influence on the plays of John Webster of tragicomedy with its clashing tones, its discontinuous characters, its ambivalent attitude toward the rhetoric it uses, the special relationship it establishes between audience and play, and its use of the mediating conclusion.

Part Two
Foreground

4
Tragedy and idle mirth: comedy and tragicomedy in The White Devil *and* The Duchess of Malfi

John Webster's introduction to his first independent tragedy, *The White Devil* (1612), admits that the play had been a box-office failure. It had been acted at the wrong time of year, and at a theatre whose house style was more suited to other, less complex, kinds of play, so that Webster's challenging new tragedy had lacked 'a full and understanding auditory' (6). More important, Webster considers the criticism that the play 'is no true dramatic poem' (13). He admits that he had dispensed with the trappings of classical tragedy, 'the sententious Chorus ... the passionate and weighty Nuntius ...' (19–20), but he also seems to feel that the play diverges from a conventional tragic norm in more crucial ways. Above all, it lacks the singlemindedness of tragedy with its consoling vision of human nobility and its earnest and lofty tone, 'height of style, and gravity of person' (18). It is not just in its diction and characters, though, that *The White Devil* fails to resemble classical tragedy. The play is a tragedy which reaches its final statement through the language and forms of comedy and tragicomedy. In his second independent tragedy, *The Duchess of Malfi* (1613), Webster seems to have attempted a more orthodox method of construction, but even this play uses comic and tragicomic methods so extensively that it has been described as a 'melodrama', a 'comitragedy', or a tragedy spoiled by 'comic and satiric confusion'.[1]

Webster of course is not alone in writing tragedies which resemble tragicomedy by presenting us with its 'genuine dilemma of feeling'.[2] Aldous Huxley called tragedy 'the literature of Partial Truth' as opposed to serious or comic epic, the literature of 'the Whole Truth'.[3] Elizabethan and Jacobean tragedies often tried to overcome this limitation by expanding to include comic anecdotes, incidents, or images.

This may take the form of isolated comic episodes, the Porter scene in *Macbeth*, or the scene in Marlowe's *Dido Queen of Carthage* (IV.5) where the old Nurse, because she is holding Cupid and not Ascanius as she believes, is made to think grotesquely lustful thoughts, a scene which parodies Dido's painful and irrational love. A character may be invented on whom a whole series of comic scenes centres, like Balurdo in Marston's *Antonio* plays. Strumbo in *Locrine* (1595) shows especially clearly the Clown's rôle as parodist. Throughout the play he undermines the themes of love and war in the main plot. His grotesque description of his love-sickness (I.2) immediately precedes Locrine's declaration of his intent to marry Guendoline, and his ludicrous battle with Margerie and her family (III.3) punctuates the serious fighting. Levels of seriousness even clash across scenes. In Act Two, scene five, Albanact's rhetorical suicide is surrounded by the fooling of the clowns: Strumbo, like Falstaff, even pretends that he has been killed and allows Trompart to speak a mock elegy over him.

The most extreme form of this juxtaposition of tones occurs in those plays which unite plots of two different kinds, tragic and tragicomic, as in Heywood's *A Woman Killed with Kindness* (1603), or tragic and comic, as in Ford's *Love's Sacrifice* (1632), or the lost *Keep the Widow Waking* (1624). In Middleton and Rowley's *The Changeling* (1622) a comic subplot about wooing and disguise set in a lunatic asylum precisely parodies the main plot in order to comment on the 'changes' which are taking place there. Comedy and tragedy, though, can interpenetrate even more closely than in the form of plot and subplot. Marlowe especially organises sharply contrasting tones in close proximity. In *The Massacre at Paris* (1593) each murder is greeted by a callous joke. In *Dr Faustus* (1592), tragedy is attacked and mocked by parodic and anti-tragic forms, and the tragic hero himself is involved in the comic scenes. Even *Tamburlaine* (1587–8) when it was first staged included 'fond and frivolous gestures' which the first printer Richard Jones omitted because he considered them 'far unmeet for the matter', merely 'deformities' designed to impress 'vain conceited fondlings'.[4] Whether these 'gestures' were the work of Marlowe or the actors, Jones was perhaps wrong to consider them irrelevant. The plays still retain strong elements of black comedy, like the Olympia episode in Part Two, or the scenes with the foolish king Mycetes in Part One. Moreover, ironic deflation remains one of the most important effects of the play. Tamburlaine's marvellous lyrical praise of Zenocrate (Pt 1, V.2.72–110) is ironically qualified by its placing immediately after his callous treatment of the Virgins of Damascus. Again, the hyperbolical laments for the dead Zenocrate ironically give way to a flat and passionless account of 'rudiments of war' (Pt 2, III.2.54). Our view even of the Marlovian superman is qualified by incongruity and ironic deflation.

This playing off against each other of tragic and anti-tragic effects is also crucial to Marston's 'seriously fantastical' tragedies,[5] to *King Lear* with its 'comedy of the grotesque',[6] to *The Revenger's Tragedy* where tragedy uses farce to express violence and terror, to *Women Beware Women* where revenge tragedy and comedy of manners clash disturbingly across the play, and to many other Elizabethan and Jacobean tragedies. The whole movement of Jacobean tragedy is toward a mixed genre which could express 'the Whole Truth'. *The White Devil* and *The Duchess of Malfi* do not exist in a vacuum. They are not unique in their admission of anti-tragic elements of comedy and tragicomedy but they do use them with unusual coherence: comedy and tragicomedy are treated not only as a threat which tragedy must face and overcome, but also as a form of real reservation about the tragic absolutes and as part of a rigorous critical double-vision.

Beaumont and Fletcher learned to write comedy and tragedy by first writing tragicomedies: Webster learned to write tragicomedy by writing comedies and tragedies. His formal tragicomedies *The Devil's Law-case* (1617), *A Cure for a Cuckold* (1625), and perhaps *The Fair Maid of the Inn* (1626) are among his latest works, while his theatrical apprenticeship was spent in collaborating on city comedies and historical tragedies. However Webster's interest in mixed forms is obvious from his earliest works. In 1604 he contributed to Marston's *The Malcontent* an induction which is both a lively piece of theatre and a perceptive commentary on the nature of Marston's 'bitter' (Ind. 42) play. In his epistolary introduction to *The White Devil*, Webster praises some playwrights whom he regards as influences on his own work. Predictably he gives first place to writers of acknowledged intellectual weight, Chapman for his 'full and heightened style' (36–7), and Jonson for his 'laboured and understanding works' (37–8). Perhaps rather surprisingly, however, he puts Beaumont and Fletcher next, before the popular playwrights Shakespeare, Heywood and Dekker, with whom Webster served his own theatrical apprenticeship. If the play was presented in about 1612, Webster must have been involved in its slow and careful composition during the period in which Beaumont and Fletcher were experimenting with various kinds of mixed form in *The Knight of the Burning Pestle* (1607), *The Faithful Shepherdess* (1608), *Philaster* (1609), and *A King and No King* (1611). For his first independent tragedy Webster had three kinds of mixed play before him: Tudor tragical comedy based on tragedy undercut or disturbed, the grotesque tragedy of *King Lear* or *The Revenger's Tragedy*, and Fletcherian tragicomedy. All three leave their mark on *The White Devil* and *The Duchess of Malfi*.

One of the most immediately striking aspects of these two plays is their close juxtaposition of extreme tones within and between scenes. In *The White Devil* Flamineo and in *The Duchess of Malfi* Bosola attack the passions of their masters and undermine their ideals of achievement and order with satire. At the first meeting of Brachiano and Vittoria their sensual, egocentric concept of love is challenged by the impotent jealousy of Camillo, the hysterical moralising of Cornelia, and the satirical commentary of Flamineo and Zanche. No scene, character or relationship is seen in only one way. This scene begins as comedy: Flamineo gulls the ridiculous Camillo with a series of dramatic double-meanings really aimed at Brachiano, and the tone of the encounter is repeatedly described as 'happy' (I.2.6, 10, 16, 205). As the scene progresses, however, it takes on the tones of tragedy: Vittoria relates the dream which will lead to two murders, and Cornelia delivers the terrible curse that Vittoria should, like Judas, betray the man she kisses (I.2.298). In the same way in *The Duchess of Malfi* the Duchess' commitment to love and its expression in her pregnancy are challenged by Bosola's satirical descriptions of her and of sexuality in general.

   This disturbing juxtaposition of clashing tones runs deeper than the constant use of satirical commentary. Brachiano in *The White Devil*, for example, is at least in part a comic character. In his first interview with his wife and her supporters his tone is at first flippant and amused – 'They are but crackers!' (III.1.73). When Florence accuses him of impropriety with Vittoria he contemptuously answers with a pun, 'Happily' (III.1.53), both 'perhaps' and 'pleasurably'. Later in this scene he also gives Isabella's excuse for her visit to Rome, 'devotion' (II.1.150), an unwelcome double meaning. At least at first Brachiano is playing a comic scene, while Isabella is acting out a 'sad . . . part' (II.1.225). So complex are the tones in this scene that even Isabella's brother Florence interprets this 'sad . . . part' only as a source of 'excellent laughter' (II.1.276). The three have nothing in common, not even the kind of play in which they see themselves taking part.

Again in *The Duchess of Malfi* the scene in which the Duchess woos Antonio seems to be basically a comic scene in which a young woman defies convention to marry the man she loves. However the comic pattern is disturbed by ominous suggestions of death and madness, by the discussion of the Duchess' last will, and by Antonio's fear of his own ambition, the 'great man's madness' (I.1.420). Even the image of the shroud coalesces with that of the sheets of the marriage-bed (I.1.389). In the disintegrating world of the play, material which comedy specifically affirms, the independence of love, fiction, art and laughter, is seen to lead directly to a tragic catastrophe. Cause and effect are dislocated as the play insists that both tragedy and comedy form essential parts of its experience.

The two plays also employ colliding tones in their use of what seems to be a particularly tragicomic device, the use of ironic repetition. This may be used to undercut the tragic status of an incident or to make its comic status increasingly uneasy, or it may ensure that we are reminded of a past episode which we are suddenly made to see as precisely relevant to the present moment of the play. In *The White Devil* especially this repetition is an important structural device. Some critics have found the play 'disjointed',[7] rich in striking incidents but weak in overall design. I would suggest rather that the play's scenes are connected by an elaborate and coherent system of parallels and repetitions, so that any scene can economically recall its past. I shall have more to say about some kinds of repetition later. At the moment I simply want to point out the importance, and the variety, of this repetition.

To a reader the most immediately striking kinds of repetition are verbal. It is well-known that the play builds up an intricate network of iterative images: animals and birds, natural disasters, poison, devils, jewels, especially counterfeit jewels. Even critics who have denied the play unity of structure have often admitted its metaphorical unity. The repetition of images, though, does not simply create a general sense of the world which the play inhabits: the process may also create links between episodes or characters, drawing the play into a tighter unity. In the first scene the violent Lodovico, banished for murder and other crimes, is taunted by his friends, who suggest that he must have been 'begotten in an earthquake' (I.1.27). In the next scene, as Cornelia watches Brachiano's seduction of her daughter, she remarks that 'violent lust' (I.2.220) is more destructive than 'earthquakes'

(I.2.218). There is no chance that we shall mistake Lodovico for the villain of the play and Brachiano and Vittoria for romantic hero and heroine. The imagery that surrounds them is too similar, and suggests that they are alike in their potential for destructive violence. Again, when Monticelso has become Pope, he tries to prevent Lodovico from committing the violence he intends. 'Come, what devil was that / That you were raising?' he asks (IV.3.88–9). In the next scene Flamineo gives an obscene twist to the same image to comment on his relationship with Zanche:

> 'Tis not so great a cunning as men think
> To raise the devil: for here's one up already,–
> The greatest cunning were to lay him down –   (V.1.88–90)

Again two different groups of characters are linked: a repeated image here indicates the similarity of lust and murder, and shows both at the roots of the play's tragic catastrophe.

Other verbal repetitions also perform the task of linking different parts of the play. Vittoria's dream (I.2.229–55) suggests to Brachiano the murders of Camillo and Isabella. Zanche also relates a dream as part of her seduction of Mulinassar (V.3.223–39). This recalls the previous seduction scene, and as in the previous scene a dream is to lead to murder. The chain of cause and effect behind the action of the play is stressed by these repetitions, and because of it the complex events of the play never become confusing. Again, when Brachiano is attempting to seduce Vittoria he tells her that, if she does not surrender to him, he will be 'lost eternally' (I.2.208). Later as Brachiano is dying amid madness and 'horror' (V.3.34), Vittoria realises that she too is now 'lost for ever' (V.3.35). Again the initial scene of seduction and plotted violence is identified as the cause of the later murders. Finally one small example can indicate how repetition can cast ironic light on an apparently straightforward detail. When Florence disguises himself as Mulinassar in order to watch his plot take effect, Flamineo tells us about the Moor's career:

> He hath by report, served the Venetian
> In Candy these twice seven years, and been chief
> In many a bold design   (V.1.9–11)

The detail here seems trivial: 'Candy' means 'Crete'. However we might notice that when Brachiano, Flamineo and Dr Julio plot the death of Camillo, Flamineo uses the word in its contemporary slang sense: 'They are sending him to Naples, but I'll send him to Candy...'

(II.1.290–1). Here 'Candy' means 'death'. In Act Five Flamineo's chance association of Florence–Mullinassar with Candy ironically predicts Flamineo's own death at the hands of the Duke's agents. Here tragicomic repetition sharpens not only the structure of the play but also one of the play's many ironies.

These repetitions, however, are by no means confined to language, but are visual as well as verbal. Certain stage images are repeated through the play. The ironic use of the kiss is one such. A conventional sign for love, it is used to register divorce (II.1.192, 253) and even as a method of murder (II.1.301, II.2.36–31). Finally to withold the kiss that might poison becomes the final sign of love (V.3.26). Hardly an act exists in isolation. In the arraignment scene, for example, Brachiano interrupts the court's ritualistic pieties by coming uninvited. Finding there is no place for him he spreads out on the floor 'a rich gown' (III.2.4 SD) and sits on it. Even this comparatively trivial act does not exist in isolation. The audience is succintly reminded of the first meeting of Brachiano and Vittoria, where Zanche spread out a carpet with cushions for the lovers (I.2.204 SD). By this apparently casual repetition we are reminded, at the beginning of Vittoria's trial, of the crime of which she is accused.

When Brachiano enters in armour to take part in the entertainment which is to prove so disastrous (V.2.44 SD) we are reminded of Giovanni's previous entrance as a 'champion' (II.1.95) while Brachiano is squabbling with Florence and Monticelso. In both scenes the military costume is part, not of real war, but of the ordinary peacetime exercise of a gentleman, but both scenes lead to real violence, verbal or physical. Two episodes of the play are once more drawn closer together. Again, at three crucial points in the play the young Giovanni is protected from danger. When at the end of the play the English Ambassador protects the prince from the escaping murderers, we are reminded of two earlier episodes. Isabella, dying, refuses to allow her son or her friends to endanger themselves by approaching her (II.2.23 SD): later the dying Brachiano orders his attendants to remove his son (V.3.16). Three crucial events are shown to be linked in the play's scheme of cause and effect. Finally in the last act Cornelia enters, insults and strikes Zanche, and abruptly leaves (V.1.185–6). This gratuitous violence on the part of his mother provides a blueprint for Flamineo's equally abrupt and startling murder of Marcello in the next scene. Flamineo enters, strikes, speaks two and a half lines, and immediately leaves. Again one event is seen as producing another with a pattern similar to its own. Webster was a notoriously slow worker: one reason for this is the extraordinary richness of the plays and his meticulousness in providing this elaborate web of cause and effect, of echo, repetition, parody and allusion.

Most striking of the uses of tragicomic repetition in *The White Devil* is the way in which almost all of the play's major incidents are repeated and parodied. The arraignment of Vittoria is closely followed by a repetition of this situation of testing as Brachiano interrogates her. Brachiano's declaration of divorce from Isabella is followed by a repetition of the scene in which she protects her husband by pretending that she herself pronounced the divorce. She closely echoes Brachiano's language but her agonised and half-ridiculous hyperbole – 'a thousand ears . . . a thousand lawyers' hands . . .' (II.1.287–8) – tips the scene over into parody. In the last scene this structure of a serious action followed by a parodic replay is inverted as Flamineo acts out a grotesque fiction of his own death, a fiction which is followed by real murder, so that a farcical image of finality and a tragic image face each other across the last scene. *The White Devil* with its elaborate system of repetition and parody, its ironic contrasts between interpretations of its events, and its insistence that every incident is intimately connected with other incidents, fits the shifting values and ironic double-visions of tragicomedy into the tragic framework of aspiration, failure, and death.

In *The White Devil* the play's system of internal repetition forms links between seemingly unlike incidents, so that a single word, image or gesture suddenly strikes a spark with the past. In *The Duchess of Malfi* this system of repetition and parody is less elaborate and less fragmented. A single incident is repeated and repeated throughout the play: the Duchess's wooing of Antonio. These reflected images of the wooing scene become increasingly grotesque and disturbing as the play progresses, so that the Duchess' secret marriage is examined and re-examined through the play. In Act Three Scene Two Ferdinand, maddened by jealousy, bursts into his sister's bedroom to confront her and her husband, and the whole scene begins to take on the form of the wooing scene. Ferdinand's gift of the poniard with its threatening phallic suggestions grimly recalls the Duchess' playful banter about the old tale in which a naked sword is placed between the two partners to keep them chaste (I.1.500–1). In the wooing scene the Duchess contrasts her living person with the effigy 'cut in alabaster' (I.1.454) upon her husband's tomb: now Ferdinand repeats this funerary imagery in his sense that the 'massy sheet of lead' (III.2.111) from the tomb of the Duchess' husband has now been wrapped about his heart. The Duchess, pretending to banish Antonio, talks of signing his 'quietus' (III.2.188), reminding us of the kiss in the wooing scene by which the Duchess gives her new husband his *'Quietus est'* (I.1.464). Again the later scene repeats the stage-patterning of the earlier as an interview is watched from concealment. At the end of the wooing scene, Antonio was startled when Cariola revealed herself. Here, badly frightened, he turns on her and accuses her of betrayal. The whole scene is an ironic reflection of the wooing scene, with love replaced by hate as its motive force. It marks an inversion, too, of some of the play's hard-won lessons about love and trust. Not only does the terrified Antonio distrust Cariola, but the Duchess even suggests that Ferdinand came to her by Antonio's 'confederacy' (III.2.88).

The wooing scene is recalled more grimly in Act Four: the Duchess's murder is ironically surrounded by echoes of the wooing scene. The imagery of funerary sculpture is repeated (IV.2.102, 156–62), the Duchess discusses the 'last will' (IV.2.200), which was her pretext for summoning Antonio to the wooing scene. Even the Masque of Madmen is a presentation in concrete form of some of the images of the wooing scene, where Antonio feared that his 'ambition' in marrying the Duchess was a kind of 'madness' (I.1.240), and Cariola suggested that her mistress was in the grip of 'a fearful madness' (I.1.506). In the wooing scene the Duchess raises Antonio from his knees (I.1.416): now she kneels to register her own humility. This web of repetition disturbingly shows madness and death operating within a frame of sanity and normality, and ironically and poignantly marks the Duchess's need for love as the force which dooms her.

Finally the wooing scene is reflected in grotesquely comic form in Julia's wooing of Bosola. Julia, who prizes love above social conventions and who dies because of that commitment, is a distorted version of the Duchess; she continues to suggest the values of the Duchess but undercuts them by her fickleness. Like the Duchess, Julia takes the active rôle by wooing the man she loves. The repeated imagery of weapons and of jewels links the two wooing scenes. These key scenes in the play, then, are developed as increasingly grotesque distortions of a single act. The Duchess's active commitment to life and to love is repeated, becoming more extreme as the society of the play, deprived of the Duchess's healing presence, falls apart into melancholy, apathy, madness and murder.

The two plays develop this tragicomic web of repetition and parody through unexpected comparisons made between characters as well as between incidents. In *The White Devil* this system of parallels is repeatedly used to undermine the tragic status of the noble characters. When Brachiano's wooing of Vittoria in the second scene is directly juxtaposed with Camillo's ludicrous courting of his own wife, it seems that the effect is a simple contrast between the impatient and passionate aristocrat and the foolish and impotent citizen. As the play progresses, though, Camillo and Brachiano come to seem increasingly alike. Camillo and Brachiano are both highly educated (II.1.30, I.2.153), but each is also a 'fool' (IV.2.142). Both are described by the emblem of the stag, a horned beast with violent sexual appetites (II.1.94, II.1.325). Both men are murdered during athletic exercises. In the second scene of the play Flamineo makes a bawdy joke about Camillo and the 'great barriers' (I.2.28–9): Brachiano's demonstration at barriers later turns into 'unfortunate revels' (V.3.8). This extended comparison deflates Brachiano's pretensions to heroic status, and shows grotesque comedy modifying even the play's treatment of romantic love.

In *The Duchess of Malfi* the comparison of characters is less fragmented and more clearly organised. I have already commented on links between Julia and the Duchess, and the murder of Cariola is deliberately posed as a parody of the death of the Duchess. Especially interesting, however, are the unexpected links which are developed between two strikingly unlike characters, Antonio and Bosola. Again we expect an absolute contrast between the Duchess's virtuous husband and the man who tortures and kills her, but again as the play progresses the two come to seem more alike. The two are linked from the first minutes of the play. Antonio first introduces Bosola and helps to control the audience's response to him (I.1.23–8, 74–82): he is on stage with Delio while Bosola first talks to the Cardinal. Both men have travelled, both have some link with France. They are associated in Ferdinand's mind (I.1.228–9). Antonio who took the ring oftenest is linked with Bosola who holds the provisorship of the horse and who gives the Duchess apricots ripened in horse-dung. At the end of the play it is Bosola who takes the part which should have been Antonio's, bringing 'comfort' (IV.1.137) to the Duchess, rebuking Ferdinand, begging the 'fair soul' (IV.2.342) to return to life, imagining himself haunted by the dead woman, and even avenging her murder. Both the plays are given coherence by these links between characters, which prevent us from making simple value-judgements. Brachiano can be no romantic hero: he is too like the ridiculous Camillo. Antonio can be no model of virtue: he is too like the equivocal Bosola.

This undermining of tragic situations and characters is one of the ways in which Webster's tragedies show the influence of Fletcherian tragicomedy. E. M. Waith suggested that Fletcher developed a new system of 'hypothetical' characters, discontinuous and multifaceted.[8] Most of the characters in *The White Devil* show this tragicomic ambiguity. All our judgements on the play's characters are constantly qualified. Marcello and Cornelia, for instance, have fine moral sensibilities, but they acquiesce in Vittoria's dubious marriage when they can profit from it. Almost every character in the play is presented in terms of antithesis and contrast. Isabella is hysterically jealous but capable of unexpected generosity. Brachiano is a noble soldier and scholar but also a 'fool' (IV.2.142). Vittoria especially is a focus for these ambiguities. She torments her husband and suggests his murder to her lover, but she defends herself from these charges with such 'innocence-resembling boldness'[9] that the whole question of guilt and innocence becomes irrelevant: in this world of shifting perspectives we are judging not moral absolutes but the quality of the performance. The dying Brachiano finally recognises her equivocal qualities, seeing her as a false steward (V.3.82–6) and an ageing adultress (V.3.117), but also as 'this good woman' (V.3.17) who deserves 'infinite worlds' (V.3.17). Like Philaster and like Arbaces, Webster's characters can be both noble and ridiculous.

Webster backs up this system of ambiguous characterisation with a series of images which insist that there is no such thing as an absolute or an objective judgement. These images of relativity stress that where we stand effects and changes the ways in which we perceive. He that has the yellow jaundice thinks that everything he sees is yellow (I.2.109–12): distorting spectacles can also change our modes of perception (I.2.100–7). Especially interesting are images of the sea-voyage in which the way we perceive is changed or distorted. Men at sea think the land is moving (I.2.156–8): ships that look very large in the river look very small at sea (V.1.117–18). Such images warn us that the world is subject to constant change, and that absolute standards and objective judgements can have little validity.

The Duchess of Malfi seems to be more conventionally tragic in its organisation, and therefore to be 'a play about character'[10] in a simpler sense than *The White Devil*. In *The White Devil* most of the characters are shifting and ambiguous. In *The Duchess of Malfi* formal character-sketches produce a more solid and less equivocal system of characterisation. People repeatedly offer these direct descriptions of the characters of others. Indeed Castruchio and Malateste exist almost solely through satirical descriptions and Pescara through laudatory comments. The Cardinal, Ferdinand and the Duchess are described in detail at the beginning of the first act, and Bosola and Ferdinand are again described in Act One Scene Three, a scene whose lack of physical action prepares for the violence to come. These character-studies produce an effect strikingly different from the shifting ambiguities of *The White Devil*. The Duchess is a simpler tragic figure than Vittoria, a woman committed to real human relationships in a world of pretence, and whose motherhood is a potent symbol attacking the sterility of her society. She is a simple character trapped in an ambiguous world, forced to assume 'masks and curtains' (III.2.159) when her own impulses would prefer frank and open demonstrations of feeling.

The Duchess is however surrounded by less simple characters, characters in whom, as in Brachiano, the tragic absolutes are questioned and undermined. Antonio is perhaps especially interesting. As the husband of the heroine we might expect a romantic hero, a Romeo or an Othello. This is not at all the character Webster has created. Antonio starts the play with a special relationship with the audience: like him, we are newcomers and outsiders at the court of Malfi, and we appreciate his descriptions of characters and situations, and his political generalisations. He is introduced first as an acute critic, then as an athlete, 'a good horseman' (I.1.140), then as a steward of integrity, 'an upright treasurer' (I.1.372), then as 'a complete man' (I.1.435). However as the play progresses his virtues are significantly undermined and this special relationship with the audience is stretched and distorted. His acute judgement and his athletic ability are both compromised by his fear, a destructive nervousness which saps his ability to make decisions and which leads to horrifying mistakes like his loss of the horoscope. 'Fear' and a desire for 'safety' at any cost become key characteristics of his in the second half of the play (e.g. II.2.74, II.3.12, III.1.18, V.1.14). Even his status as 'an upright treasurer' (I.1.372) is finally compromised as he is forced to act out the fiction of being banished for embezzlement.

As Antonio is gradually distanced from the audience and significantly reduced in stature, his function as a guide for the audience is taken over by Bosola. Antonio is torn between his fear and his love, between his ideal of 'a fixed order' (I.1.6) in society and his own infringement of that order. Bosola also is a divided character, torn between the clarity of his moral vision and his inability to do selflessly what he sees to be right. His incisive moral sense, his natural barometer for truth and falsehood, and his natural sympathy with suffering have a grotesque dark side in his inability to let moral insight dictate moral action, his own need to use fiction, and his devastating and painful satirical outbursts.

In *The White Devil* the character who speaks most directly to the audience and who helps us most to understand the ambiguous people of the play is Flamineo, who seems less discontinuous because alone of the play's characters he regularly allows us to see the workings of his mind. In *The Duchess of Malfi* the process if reversed and it is the two ambiguous commentators Antonio and Bosola who guide our responses toward a group of more conventionally conceived tragic characters.

The White Devil and *The Duchess of Malfi* share certain features of tragicomedy, the ironic use of repetition and of unexpected links between events and characters, the juxtaposition of clashing tones and definitions, and the use of shifting characters who are related to the audience through the intermediary of a commentator. Both plays use extensively and significantly a series of words which we might rather expect to find in comedy. It is not just that the two plays make much use of comic and satiric anecdotes and insets: laughter echoes through the plays, which also repeatedly use words like 'laugh', 'jest', 'merry', 'smile' and so on. Throughout the plays tragedy is tested and challenged by these reminders of comedy.

This use of the reassuring world of comedy to test and challenge tragedy is not of course unique to these two plays. When Titus Andronicus finally passes over the borderline into madness, his laughter is a symptom of his mental state (III.1.264): his breakdown is reflected in the breakdown of the genres. In *The Changeling*, after Beatrice-Joanna has bought Alsemero at a price higher than she had expected, Deflores watches her wedding procession 'smiling', when the ghost of the murdered Piracquo 'appears to Deflores in the midst of his smile' and 'startles' him, as the procession passes over the stage 'in great solemnity' (IV.1. initial SD). In *The Revenger's Tragedy* Lussurioso attempts to persuade Piato-Vindice to act as pander to

Castiza, really Vindice's sister. Lussurioso is cynically amused by the fact that the girl's own brother Hippolito recommended Piato to him: 'We may laugh at the simple age within him'. Vindice, who perceives still deeper ramifications to the irony, replies 'Ha, ha, ha' (I.3.151 ff).

Laughter may express attitudes from sympathetic involvement to callous detachment. In comedy it may express our sense of a human community: even in satirical comedy the audience as it laughs forms a social unit which is closed to the ridiculous object of that laughter. In tragedy, it carries more disturbing suggestions of aggression, detachment and isolation. At the same time laughter in tragedy may also suggest a genuinely comic world, the realm of 'the Whole Truth' which tragedy is not to enter. *The White Devil* and *The Duchess of Malfi* seem, above all Jacobean tragedies, to use laughter in order to stress the proximity of tragedy and comedy, to extend the tragedy, and to present rivals to its 'Partial Truth'.

The White Devil uses laughter and the vocabulary of comedy most extensively of all Webster's plays, testing every stage of the tragic experience against them.[11] The 'paradoxical figure'[12] of laughter haunts the play: thirteen times in this tragedy a character laughs or describes his situation in terms of laughter. Flamineo predictably attracts laughter: he is an opponent and challenger of the values and of the solemnity of tragedy, and his laughter reinforces his numerous witty anecdotes and conceits, jokes and satirical set-speeches, and his 'ridiculous . . . varying of shapes' (IV.2.243–6). However hardly a character or situation is completely distanced from laughter or suggestions of comedy. In a particularly nasty example Isabella's murderers, after poisoning the picture of Brachiano, 'depart laughing' (II.2.23 SD). Brachiano especially is attacked by laughter, as befits a tragic hero who is also a fool and who tries to impose a comic interpretation on the sufferings of others. His flippancy in his first meeting with Isabella contrasts with her agony, and even in the arraignment scene he enters, treats the scene as a comedy, makes a few jokes, loses his temper, and leaves Vittoria to fend for herself. Where his own passions are uninvolved, he sees nothing but comedy. It is all too appropriate that the death-scene of this man, who was unable to take suffering seriously, should be surrounded by disquieting images of comedy, haunted by puns and by Brachiano's own laughter, a horrible echo of the laughter of Isabella's murderers.

The scene which makes most use of laughter, satire and suggestions of comedy is the third scene of Act Three. Flamineo and Lodovico temporarily join forces, two malcontent-satirists commenting on a world of corruption, injustice, and decay. Finally the new allies quarrel and part with a violence fraught with comic undertones: 'I spoke that laughing ... This laughter scurvily becomes your face ... Now I laugh too' (III.3.112, 122, 124). A scene rich in satirical comedy, this separates two important tragic scenes, the arraignment of Vittoria and Florence's plotting of his revenge. Like the arraignment of Vittoria, it develops as a consciously staged episode, a comic scene which is sectioned off from its surroundings: 'Mark this strange encounter' (III.3.65). However even this satirical comedy falls into the shapes of grotesque violence which mould the play: the last chance to allow comedy to decide the play's course fails, and from this point disaster seems inevitable.

Apart from this last-ditch attempt to reassert comedy as the play's norm, laughter is most important in the most obviously tragic scenes, the first scene of Act Two where Brachiano meets Isabella and plots her murder, Brachiano's own death, and the final scene, where Flamineo chooses to 'laugh' rather than to die 'whining' (V.3.194–5). Webster deliberately creates a dichotomy between an event and the reaction to it. Murder is greeted by laughter, a tragedy of revenge must include 'some idle mirth' (IV.1.119), Lodovico's enemies 'laugh' at his misery (I.1.24), the machiavel makes his victims 'die laughing' (V.3.196), and even Florence sees his sister's agony only as a potential source of 'excellent laughter' (II.1.276). *The White Devil* uses both tragedy and comedy to evoke a world where the ordinary logic of existence is splintered, where pain is greeted by laughter and jokes form the prologue to murder.

The White Devil uses laughter and the vocabulary of comedy to allow tragedy to tell us 'the Whole Truth' and to depict a breakdown in experience which allows suffering to produce a comic response and comic action to lead to tragedy. Tragedy and comedy are not at odds: there seems little effective difference between them, since both spring from violence and pain, and the most tragic moments are on the whole also the most comic. In *The Duchess of Malfi* comedy and tragedy are antithetical, significantly organised so that they oppose each other. *The White Devil* is permeated with the language and structures of comedy, and almost every character and scene uses the comic vocabulary. *The Duchess of Malfi* uses laughter rather less extensively,[13] and verbal and structural suggestions of comedy are rather less evenly spread. They cluster around obviously comic centres, the court amusements in the first scene, Bosola's satirical monologues and his 'jest' (II.1.140) with the apricots, the grotesque comedy which surrounds Ferdinand and the Cardinal in the last scene. The vocabulary of comedy, however, is by far at its densest in the first act: the world of the play is immediately established as one in which laughter is a normal part of life, a world of people with a common ground who can share jokes and discussion, who have a common interest in moral and intellectual judgements and a common medium for expressing them. However unlike *The White Devil* the play at each stage undermines and criticises its comic elements by suggesting that far from telling us the whole truth about the play they are instead narrowly satirical, destructive and anarchic, and comedy poses a threat to the tragic experience rather than contributing to it.

The first scene is at the centre of the play's discussion of comedy and its hostile definition of laughter. The play's moral judgements, less equivocal than those of *The White Devil*, are reflected in the placing of its characters according to their attitude to comedy. Ferdinand is the leader of the faction which supports satirical comedy. Throughout the play he is associated with laughter in its most hostile and reductive form: he 'laughs / Like a deadly cannon' (III.3.54–5). His devotion to laughter is a sign of his cruel aggression. His 'mirth is merely outside' (I.1.170), a means 'to laugh / All honesty out of fashion' (I.1.171–2). He insists on his own mastery of a grim and brutal comedy, staging the horrible joke with the dead man's hand, or writing punning letters to the Duchess. He makes bawdy jokes and puns and then insists that he had not meant them to be bawdy: it is not just the tongue that 'hath ne'er a bone in't' (I.1.337), and although he denies it his discussion of horsemanship is heavy with sexual innuendo. He asserts his dominance by stilling the bawdy laughter of his courtiers with an assertion of his own absolute power over comedy: 'Why do you laugh? Methinks you that are courtiers should . . . laugh when I laugh, were the subject never so witty' (I.1.122–5). His attitude to laughter is also a sign of his detachment from real human relationships. When he seeks the most potent possible image of the way in which he feels that the Duchess has excluded him from her love, he imagines that he can 'see her, laughing' (II.5.38). This sense of disintegration, the act of laughter divorced from its comic context, sight divorced from sound, implies Ferdinand's inability to see the world as it is, and to fit its clashing elements into a coherent whole.

Laughter as a guide to characters is more important here than in

The White Devil, where almost all the characters are touched by comedy and satire. Ferdinand and Bosola use a reductive satirical comedy, in the final act the Cardinal is trapped in dangerous farce, and even Antonio is touched by this violent comedy as he plays on his wife a small practical joke which is intended to make her 'angry' (III.2.57), a joke which has disastrous consequences. On the whole the women in the play oppose this aggressive, self-assertive comedy with a seriousness or a tender humour. Julia is immediately opposed to the comedy of the men. Whereas Ferdinand is ready to 'laugh' at Castruchio's dumb idiot (1.1.129), she cannot 'abide' him, 'nor . . . to be in merry company' (I.1.133). Julia the great woman of pleasure is perhaps rather humourless. The Duchess, however, does respond to comedy, toning down its language to remove the cruelty and threat implied in Ferdinand's use of it. She determines to make her will 'smiling' (I.1.378), she accepts Bosola's 'jest' (II.1.140) with the apricots, she stands up to and defeats his satirical attack of women and sexuality, she rejoices to be 'so merry' with Antonio (III.5.53), and she determines to be 'a little merry' (IV.2.151) even with her executioners. Finally her death is posed as a contest between her own confidence in the tragic and comic absolutes and the cruel comedy of madness and despair with which Ferdinand attacks her. The Masque of Madmen is intended to force her 'to laugh' (IV.2.421) at the misery of others. The Duchess however can use even this source of cruel comedy for a positive purpose, to keep her in her 'right wits' (IV.2.6). Having defeated these last threats posed by satire, farce and melodrama, she can face death asserting the simpler values of tragic commitment and of wit and humour.

The use of comedy, then, is rather different in *The White Devil* and *The Duchess of Malfi*. In the later play the comic language is used less extensively and with greater hostility. In *The White Devil*, a play whose effect is moulded by distancing and detachment, we view the action largely through the characters who use comedy and comedy and tragedy become almost indistinguishable. In *The Duchess of Malfi*, whose effect depends on involving as well as distancing us, characters condemn themselves by the way they use comedy, and comedy and tragedy are antithetical. Like *The White Devil*, *The Duchess of Malfi* includes comic, tragicomic and farcical incidents, but again these are rather more muted than in the earlier tragedy. The comic dialogues and anecdotes are all in a low key and have the rather crude flippancy or facetiousness of real conversation. Moreover comic dialogue and anecdote tend to centre not on the main characters, as is often the case in *The White Devil*, but rather on characters on the fringe of the action, like Castruchio or Malateste. *The White Devil* makes satire tell the truth about the treacherous and corrupt world of the play, about the ambition of Flamineo or the passion of Brachiano. In *The Duchess of Malfi* satire presents only a partial and distorted view of a world touched by the values of the Duchess: Bosola's attacks on women and his stress on physical corruption is only part of the story. Both plays, in rather different ways, set tragedy against a wider background.

Webster's tragedies may seem at first to have little in common with Fletcherian tragicomedy, although links can be found in the use of discontinuous characters, the undermining of tragic situations and types, and the use of outbursts of extreme emotion which quickly peter out because the emotion has no root in the situation as it really is. The histrionic lovers' quarrel in *The White Devil* (IV.2) would not be out of place in *A Wife for a Month*. Webster's two tragedies follow the Jacobean practice of extending tragedy by comic and satirical admixtures so thoroughly that they seem close to the traditions of Tudor tragical comedy. In *The Duchess of Malfi*, as in R.B.'s *Apius and Virginia*, the heroine dies well before the end of the play so that the significance of her death can be explored, and *The White Devil*, like *Apius and Virginia*, contrasts comic and tragic interpretations of the same experiences. Webster's two tragedies make a significant use of clashing tones, incidents and images, and the creation of unexpected links between events and characters. If 'tragedy deals in absolutes',[14] in these two plays Webster is experimenting with the significant addition of comedy and tragicomedy to produce a quasi-tragic form closer to his own non-absolutist interpretation of experience.

5

'A tragic sound': tragedy and anti-tragedy in The White Devil

The White Devil expands and tests a tragic structure by adding elements we might associate with tragicomedy: clashing tones, ironic repetition, ambiguity of characterisation, theatrical self-consciousness, and a critical treatment of the rhetoric it uses. Again and again the play sets up potentially tragic situations only to invert or undermine them. Even cause and effect are dislocated: murder is greeted by laughter, celebration is torn apart by violence. Scenes which seem to promise violence fizzle out – the confrontation of Lodovico and Flamineo in III.3 ends without the large-scale violence we might expect – but violence explodes out of quite ordinary situations: the murder of Marcello is horrifying in its casualness.

An important part of the play's undermining of tragedy lies in its deliberate theatrical consciousness. It is very rich in play-quotations, theatrical allusions, and images of stage and performance. 'Plot', 'act' and 'auditory', 'part', 'revels', 'tragedy' and 'tragic', are used repeatedly to remind us of the fictional nature of what we are watching.[1] Scene after scene develops as a conscious drama with performers and audience, so that we as audience can examine our own function. Almost no scene is without its audience: Flamineo and Zanche watch Brachiano woo Vittoria, Flamineo, Brachiano and the ambassadors watch Vittoria's trial, Lodovico's friends watch his confrontation with Flamineo, Brachiano's poisoning takes place in public, the enthronement of the new Pope is a public spectacle. Other theatrical images are as prominent. The first scene of Act Two, for instance, expresses the violence and uneasiness behind Brachiano's meeting with his wife through a tissue of images from ceremony and enactment. Monticelso is Florence's 'orator' (II.1.21), while Brachiano sees the scene as a 'triumph' (II.1.82) in which he himself is the baited lion. Later he divorces Isabella in the 'latest ceremony' of their love (II.1.193), and Isabella in turn performs a 'sad . . . part'

(II.1.225) as she parodies Brachiano's declaration with histrionic thoroughness. Even the murders of Camillo and Isabella are seen primarily in theatrical terms, dumb shows presented to Brachiano. This device not only limits any sympathy we might have for the suffering victims, but it also places Brachiano, and the faculty of the audience, at the centre of the scene. Cornelia's hysterical involvement, Flamineo's satirical commentary, or Brachiano's aesthetic detachment in the face of murder, are all extreme forms of our own reactions as audience. As in tragicomedy, the audience is a central character in the play.

In its early acts the play's potentially most tragic scenes are also most undermined by theatrical images. Especially loaded is the arraignment scene, which, in the printed text, is even sectioned off with a separate title like a play within the play, a miniature drama with performers and an 'auditory' (III.2.15) of ambassadors. The scene is full of images of acting. Monticelso accuses Vittoria of being a 'counterfeit' (III.2.75) and suggests that her unsavoury career should have been 'play'd a' th' stage' (III.2.249).

It is well known that Webster fills his plays with allusions to and quotations from other writers, thereby placing his own tragedies in a larger world. What has been less explored is how much, if at all, Webster intends his audience to be aware of the contexts from which he borrows his striking epigrams or analogies. The arraignment scene seems to suggest that, on some occasions at least, a knowledge of this context may add a heavily ironic weight, or may provide an analogy for the characters involved or ominously predict their future. In general, the works from which Webster borrows most widely are Sidney's *Arcadia*, the essays of Montaigne, and Sir William Alexander's Senecan closet dramas. In the arraignment scene, he turns instead to quotations from plays, and from plays more recent and popular, and especially from Jonson and Tourneur. Again Webster is intent on establishing a fictive background for Vittoria's defence: her boldness may seem like innocence, but it is rooted in falsehood.

Monticelso attacks Vittoria with theatrical images, but she does not simply allow them to be used as weapons against her. As the verdict is given she also defends herself with significant play quotations. Most important, she twice echoes Agrippina in Ben Jonson's *Sejanus*:

> If you be my accuser,
> Pray cease to be my judge.   (III.2.225–6)[2]

You must have patience,
I must first have vengeance.   (III.2.270)[3]

Vittoria, she tries to persuade us, has the high moral character of
Agrippina, and like her is innocently persecuted by the forces of
corrupt government. Like Agrippina too, she implies, she is an
aristocratic and respected woman with a noble husband.

As well as Agrippina, Vittoria creates some other fictional rôles for
herself in this scene, ironic analogues which remind us of her position
but contrast with her real moral character. She adapts a line from
Tourneur's *The Atheist's Tragedy* to identify herself with the wit and
courage, and with the moral sense in important issues, of the wayward
but attractive Sebastian: 'A rape, a rape ... Yes you have ravished
justice' (III.2.274–5).[4]

The other persona that Vittoria momentarily adopts, not this time
from drama but from historiography, is another virtuous woman
hounded by corrupt officials – Katherine of Aragon. Like this innocent
queen, she is on trial, prosecuted by a vicious Cardinal, and like
Katherine she refuses to allow her case to be obscured by proceeding in
Latin.[5] These fictional rôles, Agrippina, Sebastian and Katherine of
Aragon, provide equivalents for Vittoria's situation, and are cunningly
designed by her to sway her audience: they provide false faces which
are ironically incomplete versions of Vittoria herself.

These ironically appropriate quotations, however, are to recoil on
Vittoria instead of protecting her. Like Katherine, she loses her case
and will be confined, separated from the man she loves. More
disturbingly, she is, like Agrippina, to lose her noble husband,
poisoned under mysterious circumstances. And, as it did for Sebastian,
adultery will lead her to be stabbed to death. As it is to do in the final
act, the play here sets up ironic paradigms from other tragedies in
order to identify ways in which *The White Devil* is to be like or unlike
other kinds of tragic experience.

The play also presents its equivocal nature by its use of generic
terms like 'tragedy' and 'tragic'. When the first four acts use these
words they are tinged with irony, mockery, or even open ridicule. The
second act distances its most obviously tragic events, the murders of
Camillo and Isabella, by presenting them only in dumb show, and also
by the generic terms which they attract. The pathetic tragedy of
Isabella, who generously prevents her retinue from endangering
themselves by approaching her, is ironically surrounded by the tones

of comedy: her murderers even 'depart laughing' (II.2.23 SD). The grotesque murder of Camillo which immediately follows is, equally ironically, surrounded by more conventional tragic trappings. Marcello 'laments' (II.2.37 SD), and the magician stage-manages the scene with 'louder music', 'a tragic sound' (II.2.36–7). Again, when Florence plans his revenge, the only 'tragedy' he can imagine as having any validity in the shifting, small-scale world of the play is one with 'some idle mirth in't' (IV.1.119). In the context of the grotesque murder of Camillo, or the cold detachment of Florence, the words 'tragedy' and 'tragic' are devalued. An important part of the effect of the fifth act must consequently be to approach a new and purer definition of tragedy, a definition which will not be too simple for the complex world of the play.

Although the final act must attempt to purge the play's view of tragedy from some of this irony and mockery, its earlier scenes are still rich in conflicting tones. They include much comic material, like Zanche's wooing of Mulinassar, or Flamineo's joking with Giovanni's courtier. More important, the final act also contains the play's two included tragicomedies, significantly ordered so that they confront and test tragedy. When Flamineo has murdered his brother, the distracted Cornelia 'runs to Flamineo with her knife drawn and coming to him lets it fall' (V.2.52 SD). This incident takes on the form of a Fletcherian tragicomedy which brings Flamineo near death but saves him at the last moment. Finally, as I shall show, Flamineo's mock enactment of his own death also assumes the form of a tragicomedy of surprise which is to be cut across by the real violence of the murderous 'matachin' (V.6.169).

As well as these enacted tragicomedies, the first scenes of the fifth act also contain other tragicomic devices which test and question the tragic experience. Ironic repetition is an important part of the undermining of tragedy in the first four acts. In the first scenes of the final act the pressure from this ironic repetition becomes greater as the play falls into more grotesque tragicomic forms. Brachiano's murder especially is ironically appropriate. His murder at barriers precisely recalls, and punishes, the athletic death of Camillo, and the poison which attacks Brachiano recalls the poison 'deadlier than stibium' (II.1.285) which Flamineo promises to compound for the murder of Isabella. Vittoria's cry that the murder of her husband leaves her 'lost for ever' (V.3.35) recalls Brachiano's sense that in his love for Vittoria he is 'quite lost' (I.2.3), 'lost eternally' (I.2.208). Finally the parody of extreme unction staged by the 'Franciscans' grimly recalls their leader Francisco's nasty suggestion that Brachiano's confessor 'with all's absolution' (II.1.69) would never be able to save his soul.

An ironic and even critical view of tragedy, then, colours the first four acts, while the fifth act tries to improvise a kind of tragedy which can stand in the detached, small-scale world of the play. Tones clash disturbingly: celebrations lead to disaster, and words like 'happy' and 'revels' take on ironic connotations. The death of Brachiano, who was unable to take seriously the suffering of others, is surrounded by laughter, although he also comes belatedly to an understanding of the tragic emotions of 'pity' and 'horror' (V.3.33–4). The whole scene, moreover, becomes strongly coloured by allusions to other tragedies. Florence as the ageing Moor Mulinassar seems to be playing the part of Othello, and the mad Cornelia with her emblematic flowers obviously recalls Ophelia. Brachiano, who in his frenzy imagines he can see 'six grey rats' (V.3.123), who confuses 'deep sense with folly' (V.3.75), and who suddenly and poignantly realises the truth about his own misgovernment, seems to allude to the mad Lear.[6] After its ironic undermining of tragedy, the play now piles up tragic allusions in order to refer more clearly to tragedy and its absolutes. For Brachiano, though, tragic understanding and tragic dignity are still precarious. The hero is also a fool who dies distracted and laughing, defeated by the comedy which he had insisted on reading into the situation of others.

Brachiano fails to maintain tragic dignity. Flamineo's values are far more profoundly disturbed by the death of his master, and he is moved further in the direction of tragedy. His sudden exposure to the emotions of tragedy makes him feel that he is 'falling to pieces' (V.4.25): ironic detachment finally fails him. He becomes gradually aware of the force of the tragic emotions of pity and terror as he sees the 'piteous sight' (V.4.147) of the dead Marcello and the distracted Cornelia, and the 'terrible vision' (V.4.149) of Brachiano's ghost. Flamineo still recognises the power of the comedy of cruelty, the 'Machevillian' (V.3.193) who can make his enemies 'die laughing' (V.3.196), but he is also becoming aware of the validity of tragedy with its terror and 'compassion' (V.5.115). The last act is profoundly divided in tone. 'Happy' (V.1.3), a key word in the shattered festivity in the first scene, is increasingly attacked by the repeated 'sad' (V.3.219, 222, 223, V.4.50, 126), as comedy and tragedy face each other across the play. The final scene must clarify these conflicting tones and attempt less mocking and uncertain definitions of tragedy.

The last scene of *The White Devil* opens with the same kind of ironic double-take which is so notable earlier in the play, and which reaches a climax in Flamineo's mock enactment of his own death. Flamineo visits Vittoria "bout wordly business' (V.6.2), though thirty lines later he has performed a complete *volte-face*: 'Pray thee good woman do not trouble me / With this vain wordly business' (V.6.31–2). Flamineo, who has just been exposed to the emotions of tragedy, is now painfully divided between genres. Vittoria and Zanche suspect that he is 'drunk' (V.6.4) or 'distracted' (V.6.22): to the dignified and controlled Vittoria, the emotions of tragedy seem disordered and insane.

The first sign in this scene, however, of Flamineo's new commitment to tragedy is a very equivocal one, the improvisation of elaborate tragic fictions. He invents a situation from romantic tragedy by pretending that Brachiano had ordered the death of his wife, and he gives substance to this fabrication by quoting the dying Brachiano and by paraphrasing Vittoria's proud statement of independence from the trial scene:

> I would not live at any man's entreaty,
> Nor die at any's bidding.   (V.6.48–9)[6]

The scene strives for a new tragic identity but this continues to be undercut by tragicomic repetitions, by Flamineo's deliberate use of fiction, and by a rigorous scepticism about the rhetoric it uses. Rejecting Vittoria's highly-coloured rhetoric as only 'feminine arguments' (V.6.69), Flamineo uses a revealing simile:

> They move me
> As some in pulpits move their auditory,
> More with their exclamations than sense.   (V.6.70–2)

Again we as audience are engaged in the action. While Flamineo seems to be denying any emotional engagement in Vittoria's predicament, this image of orator and audience in fact admits the opposite. We, like Flamineo, are moved by Vittoria's performance, her 'exclamations', despite our 'sense' or moral judgements. Images of play, performer and audience are superimposed on the scene: Flamineo stands simultaneously for actor and audience as he acts out a fictive rôle and watches Vittoria's performance.

These theatrical images undermine tragedy: we are firmly allotted our rôle as audience as part of our progressive disengagement from the play and its characters. Flamineo's theatrical images also suggest a similar course of dissimulation to Vittoria and Zanche as an escape from their dangerous situation. Vittoria enters whole-heartedly into the pretence with a heavily emotional speech which comes close to parodying tragedy:

> Behold Brachiano, I that while you liv'd
> Did make a flaming altar of my heart
> To sacrifice unto you: now am ready
> To sacrifice heart and all. (V.6.33–6)

Flamineo follows Vittoria's attempt to simulate and parody tragedy with a similar attempt of his own. Pretending to attempt suicide, he has Vittoria and Zanche shoot him, intending that they should then kill themselves. This device, though, is only another fiction, 'a plot' (V.6.150) which involves us, like Vittoria's histrionic overstatement, in the 'exclamations' but not the 'sense' of tragedy. Even the audience is momentarily deceived by the physical immediacy of this enacted death, so that our discovery of the truth forms a tragicomic surprise of great power. The mock-death forms a posed tragicomedy through which Flamineo finally expresses and exorcises the play's anti-tragic elements, and thereby purifies the tragic effect of the end of the play. The mock-death is immediately confronted by murder in earnest, and the two are precisely contrasted. The mock-death is associated with comic and parodic visions of hell and purgatory ('O Lucian thy ridiculous purgatory!' V.6.107), of pain ('There's a plumber laying pipes in my guts' V.6.144), of guilt ('What villainies thou hast acted' V.6.130–1), and of disorientation ('The way's dark and horrid, I cannot see' V.6.138). His real death ironically inverts these expected associations with its contrasting images of heaven ('I will carry my own commendations thither' V.6.197), of stoic fortitude in the face of pain ('Search my wound deeper' V.6.238), and by an undefined sense that the guilt of his life is somehow redeemed by the 'goodness' (V.6.269) – whatever that word means in this context – of his death. The sense of disorientation at Flamineo's real death, though, is no less profound – 'I am in a mist' (V.6.260). These two colliding death-scenes provide the play's final tragicomic contrast. Tragic and anti-tragic responses face each other across the play, expressing its shifting and uncertain world.

I have already suggested that in a tragicomedy like *A King and No*

King the final surprise shatters the established relationship of audience and play. Flamineo's enacted tragicomedy has a similar function. Throughout the play we have seen its events largely through Flamineo's eyes. He has had a particularly intimate relationship with the audience, confiding to us his plans, feelings and motives, warning us when he is involved in deception or disguise, and criticising for us the rhetoric of the play. He has even stood for the audience, watching Brachiano's wooing or the grief of Cornelia. The surprise of his tragicomic 'plot', a fine comic moment charged with menace, marks our growing disengagement from him. He is only an actor involved in a fiction of tragedy: the identity which the actor normally sheds as the curtain finally goes down Flamineo begins to shed rather earlier. In tragedy we might expect our relationship with the central character to grow more intense as his end approaches: here it is the growing disengagement of tragicomedy which heralds the tragic ending.

A repeated pattern in *The White Devil* is that of a serious action followed by its parody. Brachiano's wooing of Vittoria is followed by Camillo's parodic wooing, his divorce of Isabella is repeated and distorted by her. The play piles up ironic repetitions so that human dignity and seriousness are mocked and deflated. Here in the final act the pattern is reversed: dignity and seriousness can be born even in this complex and shifting world. Flamineo's enacted death with its Fletcherian structure provides a prelude to tragedy, a test for tragedy, and a means of releasing tragedy from intrusive elements of comedy and tragicomedy.

Flamineo's deliberately staged tragicomic fiction is starkly confronted by the entrance of the murderers. Flamineo's cry 'False keys i' th' court!' (V.6.168) echoes his exclamation 'Strike i' th' court!' (V.1.186) when Cornelia's attack on Zanche sets off a trail of catastrophes: we are again reminded by repetition of the sequence of cause and effect which leads up to tragedy. Like Flamineo's 'plot', the final murders are introduced by images of fiction and enactment. His vision blurred by his own exercise in fiction, Flamineo is momentarily uncertain about what is fiction and what is fact: 'Churchmen turned revellers' (V.6.170) bring 'a masque', 'a matachin' (V.6.169). Throughout the play celebration has a disquieting habit of collapsing into violence: at the inauguration of the new Pope, Lodovico is confirmed in his murderous intentions, the celebrations for Vittoria's wedding turn into 'unfortunate revels' (V.3.8). Here the Masque of Churchmen which leads to murder repeats the play's ironic suggestion that violence and celebration – especially religious celebration – are intimately connected. As the masquers 'throw off their disguises' (V.6.172 SD) the play finally abandons these images of fiction and theatricality: tragicomedy gives way to tragedy for the last time.

The White Devil, then, presents a series of anti-tragedies, ironically inverted or incomplete versions of the tragic experience: Camillo and Isabella are murdered in dumb show, Brachiano dies distracted and laughing, Marcello is killed with horrifying casualness, Flamineo stages a tragicomic fiction of his own death. These anti-tragedies are poised to allow and to emphasise the laborious and painful achievement of tragedy by Flamineo and Vittoria. Their murders are staged in slow-motion, like that of the Duchess of Malfi, to allow the self-assessment and the insistence on the integrity of one's own identity which we expect of tragedy.

Brachiano is destroyed by the sinister laughter which surrounds his murder. Flamineo and Vittoria on the other hand express their own control through purposive flippancy and black comedy: 'Of all axioms this shall win the prize: / 'Tis better to be fortunate than wise' (V.6.181–2), ''Twas a manly blow – / The next thou giv'st, murder some sucking infant, / And then thou wilt be famous' (V.6.232–4), 'I have caught / An everlasting cold' (V.6.271). It is the wit of the victims which dominates this final scene. Lodovico recalls his last meeting with Flamineo – 'Sirrah you did strike me once' (V.6.190) – a meeting which was surrounded by laughter. Flamineo now asserts his control by echoing this self-assertive, self-mocking laughter. Lodovico is nonplussed: 'Dost laugh?' (V.6.194) he asks. The images of mad laughter which surround the death of Brachiano helped to destroy the fragile tragic effect. Here the process is reversed as Flamineo expresses tragic self-assertion partly in terms of purposive flippancy and laughter.

Vittoria's achievement of tragic self-assertion is rather different from her brother's. At first she tries to use her feminine wiles on the murderers and only when this is obviously futile does she adopt Flamineo's courage and witty defiance. She too can use tough flippancy to insist on her own power, but she is also for the first time surrounded by the tragic emotions 'pity' (V.6.183) and 'fear' (V.6.222). Her self-assessment, like Flamineo's, honestly expresses itself in images of disorientation:

My soul, like to a ship in a black storm,
Is driven I know not whither.   (V.6.248–9)

However she also comes to accept the validity of conventional moral judgements, at last rejecting the values of 'the court' (V.6.261) and the 'great man' (V.6.262). Punningly she also recognises her own sinfulness and the justice of her own death:

> My greatest sin lay in my blood,
> Now my blood pays for 't.   (V.6.240–1)

Flamineo however continues to probe and to reject such conventional moral judgements. Throughout the play Webster has depicted the moral ambiguities of the play world by giving evaluative words a complex range of meanings and connotations: 'justice', 'charity', 'honour', 'virtuous', 'noble' and so on are undermined by ambiguities so that they come to seem increasingly discredited.[7] Cornelia, interrupting the adulterous encounter of Vittoria and Brachiano, urges them not to imperil their 'honours' (I.2.278) by this liaison. Flamineo picks up the word and cynically redefines it: to him it lacks 'honour' not to commit adultery but 'to send a duke home without e'er a man' (I.2.310). In the complex and amoral world of the play even these evaluative terms reveal insoluble ambiguities. In the final scene Vittoria tries to reinstate moral simplicities, but Flamineo continues to reject them, attempting rather to remake the moral absolutes. He admits that he is one of those who 'do ill' (V.6.179) and he describes his life as 'a black charnel' (V.6.270), but at the same time he suggests that his violent life is somehow redeemed by the 'goodness' (V.6.269) of his death. A moral term is redefined as has so often happened earlier in the play. Finally the moral clichés of society do not count: the closest we can get to 'goodness' in the shifting and corrupt world of the play is courage, wit, and lack of illusion. For Flamineo, moral teaching or divine revelation seems to confuse rather than clarify our view of the world:

> While we look up to heaven, we confound
> Knowledge with knowledge.   (V.6.259–60)

His rejection of moral clichés also allows him to be reconciled with his sister. As he reminds her, 'many glorious women' famed 'for masculine virtue' have in reality been 'vicious' (V.6.244–5). Vittoria's own vibrant femininity at least had its own courage and integrity.

The elaborate fictions in which Flamineo has so recently been engaged are now rejected in favour of a total agnosticism: 'O I am in a mist' (V.6.260). He deliberately shuts off past and future, thinking only of 'nothing' (V.6.202), 'I remember nothing' (V.6.204). Even language, of which Flamineo has been such a master, also turns out finally to be deceptive or pointless. The whole play has treated its rhetoric sceptically, even to the point, as I have shown, of ironically redefining evaluative words. The linguistic excesses of the ridiculous lawyer in the trial scene casts doubt on the validity of Monticelso's, and Vittoria's, rhetoric. Even in the final act Zanche's intention to speak to Mulinassar 'in our own language' (V.1.96) suggests, for a moment, that Florence's disguise might be discovered and disaster averted, but again language fails and there is no further mention of the plan. In the final scene language has become entirely untrustworthy. In the face of the 'long silence' (V.6.203) of death words have no meaning: 'to prate were idle' (V.6.204), and wisdom, moral judgements and even language are reduced to 'nothing' (V.6.202, 204, 205) by death.

Out of the anti-tragedies of *The White Devil* an authentic tragic voice emerges, purified by contrast with the preceding satiric and tragicomic detail. Vittoria makes a tragic self-assertion by accepting her own guilt and the validity of society's moral code, Flamineo by rejecting his versatility with fictions, language and Machiavellian wisdom, by continuing to make teasing moral redefinitions, and by facing, with courage and humour, the entire meaninglessness of the dark world around them.

However the play does not end with Flamineo's achievement of tragedy by using the opposing tones of satire and tragicomedy. A more conventional imposition of justice is to follow, a cooler, more detached comment on the passionate self-absorption of tragedy. Just as Lodovico surprised Vittoria and her brother, the murderers are themselves surprised by the representatives of law and order. The English Ambassador, who throughout the play represents moderation and sanity, brings about the final reordering as he keeps the young prince Giovanni back from the violent scene. For the third time in the play the young prince is protected from violence and horror. We are inevitably reminded of those previous times, at the murder of Isabella and at the murder of Brachiano, two events which started the train of cause and effect which leads to the tragic conclusion. Giovanni remains aloof and uninvolved. The play moves from the passionate individuality of tragedy to a more ordered, less dangerous world.

Like the dying Flamineo, the captured Lodovico asserts his proud self-sufficiency and insists on the irrelevance of society's moral judgements: what he has committed is a 'most noble deed' (V.6.280), an inversion of moral values which recalls and parodies Flamineo's redefinition of 'goodness' (V.6.269). He insists moreover that he has acted, at least indirectly, on Giovanni's own authority, a disturbing undermining of the play's final image of order. Giovanni as the voice of conventional morality flatly refuses this implied blame, insisting on his own ability to dispense 'justice' (V.6.292). Lodovico however still refuses to accept the validity of this justice. He continues to see what he has done only as an enacted fiction, an 'act' (V.6.293), the 'night-piece' (V.6.297) which was his 'best' (V.6.297), and which he continues to judge in aesthetic rather than moral terms.

Flamineo welcomed 'rest' from a world of 'pain' (V.6.274): Lodovico also finds 'rest' (V.6.296), even in the face of torture and death, in his own anarchic achievement. The fate of Lodovico forms a parody of the death of Flamineo, and it repeats some of Flamineo's last words but turns them upside down: Flamineo rejects fictions, Lodovico maintains them. The play presents a number of near-tragedies and anti-tragedies in which the tragic experience is inverted or fragmented. Lodovico asserts only a callous indifference to pain, Isabella only pathos and a generous disinterest, Brachiano only mad terror and despair. Only Flamineo and Vittoria precariously hold together the elements of tragedy, and after their deaths tragic stability falls apart into irony and anti-tragedy.

In a play in which order and hierarchy have themselves seemed threatening, where great men are 'violent thunder' (I.1.11), whirlpools (IV.2.70), wolves (I.1.8), eagles (V.4.6) or devils (IV.2.59), there is small comfort in the restoration of order by these great men. Even the young Giovanni may be one of these destructive great men in embryo. Lodovico loads him with blame for the murders. Flamineo has already suggested that he is another wolf or eagle whose 'long tallants . . . will grow out in time' (V.4.8–9). Giovanni's conventional appeal to 'justice' (V.6.292) may ring slightly hollow after Flamineo has redefined 'justice' (V.6.175) as his own right to kill his treacherous sister. Lodovico's assignment of blame to Giovanni, Flamineo's description of the prince's character, and the prince's own use of discredited moral clichés all serve to qualify ironically the restoration of order. Even in its final act *The White Devil* can present the affirmation of tragedy only surrounded by ironically inverted or incomplete anti-tragedies, and by constant qualifications and ambuigities.

Both of Webster's tragedies have presented critics with serious problems about their unity: *The White Devil* has often been seen as confused or disjointed. Its placing of tragedy, however, in a context of untragic and anti-tragic material is significant and deliberate. Webster's introduction stresses the unconventional form of the play, 'no true dramatic poem' (13). Not only does it use more extensively than any of Webster's other plays the language of comedy: most of its events are also surrounded and undermined by ironic commentary, ironic repetition, and images of theatricality. Webster deliberately presents a complex and shifting world which can be described only in these terms, a world without certainties, where moral terms are ironically redefined, and are expressed in ambiguities and images of relativity. The play establishes a series of double-visions where death and laughter, tragedy and comedy, are drawn into the closest possible proximity. Even the final act surrounds the tragic affirmation of Flamineo and Vittoria with a number of anti-tragedies which invert this affirmation, or show it achieved only incompletely, like the murders of Marcello and Brachiano, Cornelia's attack on Flamineo, or the capture of Lodovico. Most theatrically audacious is Flamineo's mock enactment of his own death. The final act piles up allusions to other, especially Shakespearian, tragedies which provide contrast and comparison for the ironic tragedy of *The White Devil*. In the final scene the structures of tragedy with 'pity' (V.6.183) and 'fear' (V.6.222), self-assertion and affirmation, spring out of the tragicomic context of the play with its fragmented, inverted and ironic images of tragedy. Throughout his plays, Webster has strong reservations about the ability of any simple genre to depict the complex world. In *The White Devil* this world, after false starts, reaches tragedy. In Webster's next play, *The Duchess of Malfi*, tragedy is again poignantly and precariously achieved, but here Webster is more interested in the aftermath of tragedy, and the failure of tragedy in a world without a centre.

6

'To behold my tragedy: tragedy and anti-tragedy in The Duchess of Malfi

The failure of *The White Devil* in 1612 seems to have caused Webster to re-evaluate his own view of tragedy and its relationship with other dramatic genres. Certain methods of construction remain, clashing tones, the use of satirical commentary and ironic repetition, but differences between the plays are perhaps more striking. *The Duchess of Malfi* makes little use of the moral redefinitions of *The White Devil*: good and evil are more clearly meaningful, and ambiguity less an expression of the real nature of the world than an evasion. The Duchess is a far less ambiguous heroine than Vittoria, a good woman who is forced by the threatening society around her into an equivocal situation, hiding behind 'masks and curtains' (III.2.159) when she would prefer frank and open demonstrations of feeling, expressing herself 'in riddles and in dreams' (I.1.446) when she would prefer to speak clearly and unambiguously. *The White Devil* is centred on ambiguous characters, the later play on more obviously tragic figures, a great lady who loves too well and is murdered at the instigation of her brothers. *The White Devil* from the beginning introduces tragicomic incidents, ironic undermining and the modifying use of laughter. The later play seems at least to begin as a tragedy of passion.

However *The Duchess of Malfi* has created problems about structure and unity perhaps even more seriously than *The White Devil* with its ironic repetition and deliberate fragmentation. The first four acts seem to constitute a tragedy of a palpable kind, but Webster allows his heroine to die over an act before the end of the play. *The Duchess of Malfi* begins as a tragedy and only in the fifth act confronts tragedy with satire, tragicomedy, and a distorted view of the tragic absolutes. This method of construction causes critics much uncertainty about the unity of the play. William Archer found it 'broken-backed', and Ian Scott-Kilvert finds this final act an 'anti-climax' which is 'fatal to the unity of the play'.[1] However I think this is far from our experience of the play in the theatre, and I want to examine the fifth act and its relationship with what has gone before.

The first four acts of *The Duchess of Malfi* form a coherent tragedy. Indeed tragedy seems inevitable from very early. As early as the end of the first act, Cariola defines the play as a tragedy: to her, the Duchess's wooing of her steward seems 'a fearful madness' which deserves 'pity' (I.1.506). The tragic emotions of fear and pity are already implicit in the action. As the play progresses, the tragic emotions become more pressing and inescapable. In Act Four the Duchess's torment and death are posed as a formal 'tragedy' (IV.2.8, 36, 288) scripted by Ferdinand, enacted by Bosola, centred on the Duchess, and developing in the Aristotelian combination of 'pity' (IV.1.88, 90, 95, 138, IV.2.34, 259, 273, 347) and 'terror' (IV.2.189). Where *The White Devil* uses 'tragedy' or 'tragic', it usually includes mockery or at least uncertainty of response. The fourth act of *The Duchess of Malfi* uses such words far more simply and seriously.

The tragic centre of the play is menaced by bitter comedy and by images of fiction which the Duchess must oppose with her own tragic consciousness and her acute understanding of the line dividing truth from falsehood. Bosola's disguises, Ferdinand's equivocating vow, his sinister joke with the dead man's hand, the Masque of Madmen, Cariola's desperate attempt to escape death by improvising fictions, the 'sad spectacle' (IV.1.57) of the dead Antonio and his son, which turns out to be only 'feign'd statues' (IV.2.351), the 'tedious theatre' (IV.1.84), the 'good actor' playing a 'villain's part' (IV.1.289–90), all these create a pervasive sense of fiction and unreality which can only be defeated by the Duchess's acceptance of tragedy with her eyes open, 'well awake' (IV.2.224). Tragedy is surrounded by and tested by unreality and grim comedy. It is also tested by reminders of a happy past which contrasts poignantly with the present horror. The scene, as I have already suggested, is heavy with echoes of the wooing scene. Again, Bosola's view of the Duchess as an 'unquiet bedfellow' (IV.2.140) is a poignant reminder of Cariola's banter that her mistress is 'the sprawling'st bedfellow' (III.2.13). Under attack from black comedy, from fiction, from reminders of past happiness and illusive promises of a happy future, the Duchess must laboriously salvage the tragic absolutes, insisting upon her own identity and her own clear-sightedness.

Although the Duchess preserves the status of a tragic heroine, she has an ambiguous relationship to some of the absolutes which we might expect tragedy to affirm. She chooses not to 'pray' (IV.1.95) but rather to 'curse the stars' (IV.1.96), and the world itself into 'chaos' (IV.1.99). Throughout the play the Duchess has appeared as spokesman for fruitful disorder by rejecting 'vain ceremony' (I.1.456), the traditional rôle of the nobility, and the traditionally passive rôle of women. She is contrasted with Antonio, whose conventional admiration for 'fixed order' (I.1.6) is only abandoned as he dies. Here for a moment the Duchess's acceptance of fruitful disorder almost slips over into the will for general destruction, but finally she dies in humility and 'obedience' (IV.2.169), kneeling to enter heaven, and insisting upon her own awareness and understanding, 'well awake' (IV.2.224).

The most extreme manifestation of anti-tragedy and menacing theatricality with which the Duchess is confronted is the Masque of Madmen. This masque not only attacks the Duchess: it also detaches us from the play-world by presenting a distorted version of it. The discordant music, dialogue in which no communication is made, and the ever more extreme vision of physical and spiritual degeneration reflect and comment on the play itself. The masque and its characters provide a grotesque image of the world of the play, and some of the madmen reflect quite accurately some of the play's central characters. The Third Madmen clearly recalls the Cardinal, the corrupt sensual churchman. The Fourth, the mad doctor, may reflect Ferdinand, who imagines himself as a physician treating the 'intemperate agues' (IV.1.142) of the Duchess, who sent her the grim Masque of Madmen as a 'cure' (IV.2.43), and who finally needs a doctor to treat his own madness. He himself draws the connection for us: 'Physicians are like kings' (V.2.66). The Second Madman – perhaps also the one discussed in lines 103 to 105 – is perhaps a distorted version of Bosola, who 'shows the tombs' (IV.2.102) and indulges in misogynistic and scurrilous stories of 'the glass-house' (IV.2.77, II.2.7). The Masque of Madmen, as well as presenting an attack on the Duchess by the forces of satire, also genuinely helps to keep her in her right wits by asserting her essential sanity in the face of the grotesque madness of her opponents, Ferdinand, the Cardinal, and Bosola.

This painful confrontation between tragedy and anti-tragedy is further complicated by links drawn between the representatives of the two. Bosola is not only like Antonio: he is also, in this scene, like the Duchess. The Duchess is 'like a madman' (IV.2.17), and she believes at first that Bosola is 'mad too' (IV.2.114). She compares her suffering with that of 'the tann'd galley-slave' (IV.2.28), and we recall that Bosola had served a sentence in the galleys for a murder commissioned by the Cardinal (I.1.71–3). The two are not only enemies but are also almost allies. Bosola's tissue of questions helps the Duchess to arrive at her self-definition, and his pessimism throws into relief her affirmation.

The death of the Duchess, then, is poised as the play's tragic centre, described as a 'tragedy', surrounded by 'pity' and 'terror', fighting off anti-tragedy, and finally leading to a triumphant affirmation of her own identity, 'I am Duchess of Malfi still' (IV.2.142). The Duchess is both a tragic heroine reaching a tragic affirmation, and the heroine of a tragical comedy, like R.B.'s Virginia, escaping from tragedy into a heavenly afterlife. However this posed tragedy disintegrates into anti-tragedy after the death of the Duchess. Tragedy is parodied in Cariola's high-spirited fight for life. She creates a tissue of fictions, like 'I am quick with child' (IV.2.254), which Bosola clear-sightedly recognises as fictions. Cariola is driven into subterfuge, into taking shameful ways to avoid shame. Unlike her mistress, she cannot free herself from fiction even as she dies, and the only kind of love and motherhood she can claim for herself exist in fiction only.

It is not just, then, that in Act Five the play moves away from tragedy: the Duchess' hard-won tragic moment is precarious and collapses as soon as she dies, and the return from tragedy is illustrated in several small inversions or parodies of tragedy. If Cariola parodies the tragic actors, Ferdinand parodies the tragic audience. His reaction to the death of his sister is a perversion of the tragic catharsis experienced by the audience. He first denies (IV.2.259) and then accepts the validity of tragic 'pity' (IV.2.273), sees the event as one of 'horror' (IV.2.311, 314), and interprets the whole as a 'tragedy' (IV.2.288). However for Ferdinand pity and fear are not purged: they are violently awakened, so that he rushes out 'distracted' (IV.2.336). This inversion of catharsis also brings Ferdinand to the reverse of a tragic understanding of the situation: he tries to throw all the blame on to Bosola, to imagine a fictional happy ending, and to retreat into obviously false motives and images of fiction.

At this point, with Ferdinand parodying the reactions of tragedy, in another inversion of tragedy the Duchess revives for a moment. It seems momentarily that all that has gone before is only a tragicomedy which wants deaths. For Bosola, this rich confusion of tragedy and tragicomedy poses insoluble problems. Even the tragic emotions are confused, until it seems that 'pity would destroy pity' (IV.2.347). Where the Duchess faces and accepts the truth of her situation and Ferdinand recoils from it, Bosola is faced with divided loyalties to fact and fiction, and he presents the dying Duchess with a half-real, half-unreal account of Antonio alive and reconciled to her brothers. Bosola's confrontation with tragedy leaves him still prepared to use fictions, and however kindly his motives this deliberate falsehood suggests that Bosola's dependence on fiction and deception is to shape his actions even now that he has rejected 'painted honour' (IV.2.336). Where Ferdinand retreats from tragedy, Bosola accepts it in modified form, throwing off his disguise. This acceptance, though, is complex and ambiguous. His change of direction is achieved only when he is convinced he has lost his chance for reward, so that it has a strong undercurrent of personal spite. Moreover it is a change in attitude which does not seem much to affect the way he acts, but only the people who are his friends and enemies. To see Bosola's move to the Duchess's side only as a new commitment 'to doing what he knows is morally right' or even as 'redemption'[2] seems to oversimplify. It is a strange kind of conversion which is only second choice to material advancement, and which produces the same kind of murder and betrayal as his unregenerate self.

Moreover this change in Bosola is not wholly for the good. It expresses itself not only in a discovery of his own 'guilty conscience' (IV.2.356), but also in a significant dimming of his clear moral insight. Before this he always showed a clear moral understanding even when this was rigidly excluded from his actions. From this point he no longer stands in a special relationship with the audience, he is less self-critical, and we can accept his evaluations less readily. His vow, for instance, to give the body of the Duchess to 'some good women' (IV.2.372) is made apparently without irony, although he has just participated in the murder of the play's two good women. Bosola, as he himself would have been the first to realise earlier in the play, returns as arrant knave as he set forth, because he carried himself always along with him.

The fourth act of *The Duchess of Malfi*, then, presents a tragedy in which a good woman achieves a tragic self-assertion. This tragic centre, however, emerges from a mass of anti-tragic material: a masque which provides a grotesquely distorted view of the play itself, a parody of the tragic moment as Cariola refuses tragedy and Ferdinand perverts tragic catharsis, and a miniature tragicomedy in which the

Duchess briefly revives. The act tries to suggest as richly as possible the variety of human reactions to disaster without compromising the centrality of the Duchess's positive statement. For the strong few there is the possibility of tragedy: for the majority there is only uncertainty, ambiguity, or the rejection of the difficult absolutes of tragedy. There is never any real doubt about the Duchess's courage and her essential innocence: the play's central ambiguities lie rather in the effect of her love and death on those around her. In the final scene the focus shifts from tragedy to inversions and parodies of tragedy, and from the Duchess to Bosola and Antonio. Without the tough integrity of the Duchess, tragedy falls apart into satire, self-deception, despair and madness.

Dorothea Krook sees tragedy as an interlocking sequence of four units, 'the act of shame or horror', the 'suffering' which this causes, the special 'knowledge' generated by this suffering, and the 'affirmation or reaffirmation of the dignity of the human spirit' which this new and special knowledge produces.[3] If this is a valid scheme for tragedy, *The Duchess of Malfi* seems to use the tragic framework in a peculiarly sceptical and ironic way. In the fourth act, the death of the Duchess forms a genuine tragic centre. The end of the act, and the fifth act, provide a series of inversions or parodies of the tragic scheme, in which almost all the tragic values are negated. The first three acts present an ambiguous view of the tragic 'act of shame or horror': the Duchess's unequal marriage is seen as shameful and horrifying by Ferdinand, though not necessarily by the audience. Act Four juxtaposes an authentic tragic 'knowledge' with knowledge of a more dubious kind. Act Five ends the play on an ambiguous view of tragic affirmation.

In many ways in style and in imagery Act Five is very different from the play which has gone before. The play has arranged tragedy as the peak, the highest in artistic form and in moral achievement, from which the final act charts a sharp decline. The language itself changes to emphasise this change of quality. The end of Act Four and Act Five itself are full of negatives, 'silence' (IV.2.5, V.4.83), 'never' (V.5.90), 'no' (V.5.108), 'not-being' (IV.2.301), and especially 'nothing' (IV.1.138, IV.2.15, V.2.33, 39, 54, 231, 330, 347, V.5.59, 79, 118), which echoes through the last act. After the affirmation of the Duchess's life and death the society she leaves behind her is negative and sterile.

Again in the final act the play's images of comedy and tragicomedy become more extreme and grotesque. Julia's wooing of Bosola begins as an enacted tragicomedy in which she threatens him with a pistol, and ends in tragedy in earnest, rather like Flamineo's death in *The White Devil*. The 'fatal judgement' (V.2.85) which falls on Ferdinand, the play's leading exponent of satirical comedy, is that he becomes frozen into this one posture, a comic madman afraid of his own shadow. The Cardinal too dies surrounded by laughter, doomed by the fictions which he thought he controlled.

Act Five, then, is deliberately separated from the first four acts by a change in vocabulary and by an increase in pressure from comic and tragicomic incidents. It is also separated by a change in focus on certain characters. We become increasingly distanced from the characters, and it becomes less and less easy to accept what they tell us at face value, until we can view even the last words of the play with critical objectivity. Those characters who have stood as delegates of the audience, Bosola, Antonio and the Duchess have either disappeared from the play or had this special relationship shattered. Antonio especially, who began the play by guiding our judgements, has shrunk in stature since the death of his wife. His character has fallen apart. Bosola has taken over his clear-sighted grasp of character and Delio his stubborn integrity. Only his less attractive characteristics remain, his subconscious wish for disaster, his helpless indecision, poor judgement, desire for 'any safety' (V.1.67). His death at least frees him from fear and from his conventional awe of the 'fixed order' (I.1.6) of the courtly life, which he never shakes off and which helps to doom him. Like Ferdinand and the Cardinal, he is destroyed by the death of the Duchess.

Despite Webster's deliberate use of contrasting modes in the final scenes, they are nevertheless tightly connected in theme with what has gone before. The final act might have been a second tragedy arising from the Duchess' murder, an 'act of shame or horror' which might have driven her murderers to tragic knowledge and affirmation. However in the final act, tragic structures are suggested only to be negated, inverted, or parodied, or are accepted only in a limited sense. Brooding over this series of anti-tragedies is the strongly contrasting presence of the Duchess. In a significant, almost indeed in a literal, sense the dead Duchess haunts the final act, a constant poignant reminder of a better way of living. After what seems her death she revives momentarily, she 'haunts' Bosola, perhaps even appearing as he imagines he can see her, 'there, there!' (V.2.346). She is heard again in the echo scene, and again perhaps is seen, 'a face folded in sorrow' (V.3.45). Of course she is constantly talked about in the last act, and is metaphorically present in the echoes and summaries of the past with which the ending of the play is permeated. When she appears three times after her apparent death it seems as if she and the life force which she represents are proof against death. Her tragic affirmation confronts the sceptical world left behind her, and the tragicomic discords created by this antithesis modify the effect of the final act.

Act Five contains a rich number of parodies or incomplete versions of tragedy. Deliberately fictional versions of tragedy have replaced the genuine tragedy of the Duchess: the Cardinal's quite baseless story of the ominous haunting of the family by a woman killed by her own kinsmen 'for her riches' (V.2.94) is the nearest he can get to understanding tragedy. This fabrication is a parody of the story of the Duchess: we are reminded of Ferdinand's claim that he had hoped to gain 'infinite mass of treasure by her death' (IV.2.285). The Cardinal who tries to define tragedy only in these blatantly fictional terms meets an appropriate death. He is the centre of dangerous fiction in this last act, as he uses 'fair marble colours' to conceal his 'rotten purpose' (V.2.297–8). In order to dispose of the body of Julia safely, he designs an elaborate fiction, and he warns his followers not to disturb it:

> When he's asleep, myself will rise, and feign
> Some of his mad tricks . . .
> And feign myself in danger.   (V.4.14–16)

He is also threatened by black comedy. His courtiers believe that his shouts for help are simply 'counterfeiting' (V.5.20), and they imagine how the Cardinal will 'laugh' (V.5.33) at them if they mistake his fiction for reality. By his attempt to manipulate fictions the Cardinal dooms himself, and his death provides both an exact judgement upon him and an exact inversion of the tragic process. Suffering is surrounded by comedy, knowledge brings only despair, and instead of affirming his own identity and his human dignity the Cardinal is reduced to 'a little point, a kind of nothing' (V.5.79) who only wishes to lose his sense of self and to be 'laid by, and never thought of' (V.5.90).

The Cardinal's death forms a clear anti-tragedy in which the precarious tragic moment achieved by the Duchess disintegrates. The death of Ferdinand follows the same pattern, and is also surrounded by fiction and comedy instead of dissipating them in the positives of tragedy. Ferdinand's madness is another opposite of tragic knowledge. Instead of, like the Duchess, asserting his own individuality, he imagines himself a soldier in a battle which turns into a comment on the breakdown of the family. Both Ferdinand and the Cardinal have a momentary flash of self-knowledge, but it allows them no such affirmation as the Duchess's. Ferdinand quotes Giovanni in *The White Devil* to recognise that 'Sorrow is held the eldest child of sin' (V.5.55), but he retains little sense of personal identity or personal involvement. His fate seems to him not to be his own fault, but only to be caused by the nature of the world: 'Like diamonds, we are cut with our own dust' (V.5.73). The Duchess manages to look to the future as she dies. Ferdinand can only look backwards, and the Cardinal only welcomes oblivion. Their deaths give only negative versions of the Duchess' affirmation.

The Duchess's tragedy is followed by a number of distorted versions of it which become increasingly foreign to the spirit of tragedy. Cariola resists and lies, Julia refuses to evaluate her own life, the Cardinal and Ferdinand invert and parody the achievement of tragic knowledge and affirmation. The death of Antonio is also posed as an anti-tragedy. The scene of the Duchess's murder is carefully prolonged to allow her to make her final affirmation: Antonio is killed casually and accidentally. This painfully ironic scene casts doubts on the whole possibility of just action in a post-tragic world. Bosola, who tries to commit himself to 'Penitence' (V.2.348), 'a most just revenge' (V.2.343), finds himself inescapably trapped in fictions: the murder of Antonio is seen simply as 'such a mistake as I have often seen / In a play' (V.5.95–6). Antonio's death allows the murdered man some knowledge and affirmation: at least in the face of death he finds himself able to 'appear myself' (V.4.50). However it is of so subdued a kind that it seems a parody of the Duchess's intensity. He achieves a limited kind of self-definition, but it is a weary kind which consists so largely in regret for his past deeds and the admission that throughout the play his judgement has been faulty. At the beginning of the play he praised the 'fixed order' (I.1.6) of the French court. Now he dies with a profound distrust of the ambiguous 'order' imposed by great men, wishing that his son should 'fly the courts of princes' (V.4.72). Tragedy is replaced by horrifying accident and a disturbing pessimism.

Cariola, Julia, Ferdinand, the Cardinal and Antonio is each the centre of a tiny anti-tragedy in which the values of the Duchess cannot be maintained but are inverted or distorted. The final act, though, centres on Bosola, and his anti-tragedy is the most complex of all. From the beginning of the play, of course, Bosola has been an ambiguous character: 'very valiant' but poisoned by 'want of action' (I.1.76, 80), he 'would look up to heaven' but the devil stands in his light (II.1.94–5). This ambiguity is increased rather than resolved in the final act. Like the Cardinal Bosola becomes enmeshed in fictions, despite his newly good intentions. He uses fiction with the Cardinal and Julia, but also, and this is a new development, with himself. He claims 'Penitence' (V.2.348) and uncritically claims to be taking part in a 'most just revenge' (V.2.343), apparently without recognising the irony of revenging a crime which he has himself committed. This is underlined by the ironic divergence between his intention of joining with Antonio and his accidental murder of his would-be ally.

In the final act the included incidents move further from the paradoxical calm of formal tragedy. Antonio's death is casual, ironic and muddled, Ferdinand and the Cardinal are destroyed by fiction and comedy. Finally the scene reaches the farthest stage from tragedy in the death of Bosola. Flamineo recognised some 'goodness' (*WD* V.6.269) in his death, the last of the play's many ironic inversions of value terms. Bosola similarly believes it can do him 'no harm . . . to die / In so good a quarrel' (V.5.99–100). His play has not, however, like *The White Devil* established this kind of moral inversion as a valid way of summing up a perverse and divided world. Bosola's redefinition of the adjective 'good' seems less convincing, an uncritical shifting of responsibility which is the opposite of tragic knowledge. This sense of his own rightness is deeply undermined by the accidental murder of Antonio and the casual murder of his servant, by the stress placed on Bosola's grudging sense of being 'neglected' (V.5.87) which lingers to the very end of his life, and by images of uncertainty and of fiction, 'in a mist' (V.5.94), 'in a play' (V.5.96). Bosola's definition of himself as a justified avenger is also cut across by the brutally simple summing up of his career by Malateste, 'Thou wretched thing of blood' (V.5.94).

The final irony in this ironic play is the untrustworthy nature of its last words, which we are forced to regard critically and with detachment: the affirmation of the Duchess's death is dissipated in facile pessimism and incomprehension. Flamineo's critical agnosticism in the face of death sums up the whole effect of his agnostic play. Bosola's does not: the affirmative tragic action of the play which precedes undermines his narrow and conventional stoic sentiments. He insists that men are only 'dead walls or vaulted graves, / That ruin'd yields no echo' (V.5.97–8). However we are forced to question this reductive view of human life by remembering that we have just heard the Duchess's grave returning an echo in a literal sense. Again, Bosola speaks of the 'deep pit of darkness' in which mankind lives, 'womanish and fearful' (V.5.101–2). This quotation from Sidney's *Arcadia*[4] seems to have been altered specifically to create ambiguity about the adjective 'womanish', when the play's heroine has been anything but 'fearful', and has died refusing to see the world as only a 'pit of darkness'. Bosola's flip pessimism is discredited by our memory of what has gone before: a world that has produced the Duchess and been coloured by her values might seem to be more than simply a pit of darkness. Bosola's two most negative definitions of human life, therefore, are negated by their context, but this ambiguous and indirect affirmation is the only one which the final act of the play has to offer. Finally Bosola urges 'worthy minds' not to fear death in the service of 'what is just' (V.5.103–4). This final attempt at affirmation, however, is qualified at the last moment by the sudden insight that he himself is not one of these worthy minds whose death will allow tragic affirmation: 'Mine is another voyage' (V.5.105).

Bosola's death, like all the other deaths in this final act, provides an ironic inversion of tragedy with ambiguous knowledge and affirmation. The whole scene, too, takes on the shape of these ironic verisons of tragedy. Even Delio's last lines, presented to us as a final summary, turn out to be ironically undercut. Delio attempts to redefine greatness and to sum up the play's suggestions that greatness lies not in birth or power but in moral excellence. The play's 'great men' (V.5.118) Ferdinand and the Cardinal have lost their identity as completely as footprints melting with melting snow. Men are truly 'great' only when they are 'lords of truth' (V.5.119). Only 'integrity of life', a complete and moral life, leads to immortal 'fame' (V.5.120). The Duchess, like the heroine of a tragical comedy, is assured of some kind of immortality because of her intensity and her goodness. However if Webster intended his audience to be aware of the source of his quotation it could only add disquieting ironies to what might seem a conventional summing up. Horace's ode which begins 'Integer vitae . . .' (*Odes* 1, xxii) praises the man of perfect purity and innocence. His goodness protects him even from physical danger, for even the savage wolf will not attack the truly virtuous man. In Webster's play, however, even the Duchess's 'integrity of life' cannot protect her, her husband or her children, from Ferdinand the wolf. The play's last lines which seem to offer a 'reaffirmation' turn out to be complex and ambiguous, and so does the play's vision of the future. Antonio's son is to become Duke 'in's mother's right' (V.5.113), and we might think that this is a restoration of political and moral order. However the real heir is, as Webster clearly points out to us earlier in the play (III.3.69–71), the Duchess's son by her first marriage, and this child of Antonio's who seems poised to re-establish order is the child whose horoscope predicted a 'short life' and a 'violent death' (II.3.63), and whom Antonio wished to 'fly the courts of princes' (V.4.73). Even the play's final restoration of order, then, is profoundly ironic. The Duchess's tragedy is posed at the summit of a descending scale, and the play returns from this height to the confusions, ironies and uncertainties of our real life.

The Duchess of Malfi seems to me not to be broken-backed or confused but to establish a significant relationship between tragedy and other kinds of experience. Comic, satiric and tragicomic elements are posed to define tragedy objectively and to place the tragic affirmation of a heroic individual in the perspective of an anti-heroic society. Fletcher's definition of tragicomedy made clear the kind of play he was *not* writing, that which mixed 'mirth and killing' and which included both violence and festivity, 'laughing together'.[5] This is, however, exactly the kind of play that Webster is writing in *The Duchess of Malfi*, where tragic affirmation defeats comedy and satire but is refused by an unheroic society which rejects the tragic values of the Duchess, wilfully misunderstands them, fails to live up to them, or fatally misinterprets them. Tragedy has learned to tell the Whole Truth. *The White Devil* and *The Duchess of Malfi* include miniature tragicomedies and ironically qualify tragedy: after this in his career Webster specialised in formal tragicomedy, with *The Devil's Law-case* (1617) and *A Cure for a Cuckold* (1625).

Grace . . . in action: tragicomedy in The Devil's Law-case

Although *The Devil's Law-case* does at last reach a happy ending, its world is recognisably the world of the tragedies only slightly modified. More urban and bourgeois than the tragedies, it replaces ducal or papal ceremony and the courtly life with a world of merchants, lawyers and doctors, the Exchange and the law court, and with a grasp of the economic bases of life in society. Aristocrats like Ercole and the 'great lord' (I.1.26) Contarino do enter this world, but the position at least of the weak Contarino is a vulnerable and equivocal one. He is selling his inheritance of land for money and is considering an alliance with a wealthy city family, which contribute to a series of ominous images of social change and disorder in the play's first acts. Alongside this analytic view of society runs a series of references to recent history or contemporary affairs, especially disturbing references to disorder, violence and betrayal: the fatal misunderstanding between Elizabeth and Essex (III.3.271–5), the Gunpowder Plot (IV.2.287), the clashes between the British and the Dutch in the East Indies (IV.2.10–11), the Battle of Lepanto (IV.2.334), the loss of Calais (IV.2.397), great frosts and plagues (IV.2.396). These images throng especially around the trial scene where Leonora tries to prove that her own son is a bastard, creating an appropriate background for the violence and betrayal that take place there. This dense field of contemporary reference and a firm stress on the economic and hierarchical aspects of society create a world recognisably like our own, and form a strong contrast with much that is fantastic or unlikely in the play, only the first of a number of striking and extreme contrasts, tragicomic discords, through which the play operates.

Apart from this greater stress on commerce, on social distinctions, and on contemporary affairs, *The Devil's Law-case* makes much use of images, motifs and situations drawn in part from the earlier tragedies. The central character Romelio is recognisably akin to Flamineo, witty, unscrupulous and self-seeking, trying to compel his sister to act in ways which advance him. Romelio is a 'merchant' both literally and in the contemporary slang sense of a rascal (III.2.7). *The Duchess of Malfi* centres on a 'young widow' (I.1.457) who decides to marry. Leonora in *The Devil's Law-case* is an elderly widow painfully in love with a young man whom her daughter also loves. Like *The White Devil*, *The Devil's Law-case* includes a trial scene in which through lies and deceptions the true nature of some of the characters becomes clear. In some ways, indeed, the world of *The Devil's Law-case* seems rather darker even than that of the tragedies. It is a world grown older: Romelio himself is thirty-eight, and his mother Leonora fights desperately against society, time, and her own daughter to have her 'last merriment 'fore winter' (III.3.251) with the young Contarino whom she loves. The play's happy ending is drawn out of grief and pain and the fear of old age, and it recalls the tragedies in its images of madness, hell and the devil. Although Jacobean tragicomedy resembles comedy in its structure and in the final achievement of the happy ending, the material which fills out this structure can vary very widely in tone and colouring. In *The Devil's Law-case* tragedy provides a particularly challenging opposition.

However despite its sombreness the play insists on its own comic identity. The word 'comical' even appears twice in the last act, as the characters welcome 'these so comical events' (V.6.62) after the fear and danger of the play. Set comic turns, however, involve the main characters far less than they do in the earlier plays. In *The White Devil* Vittoria's trial is introduced by a comic scene in which Flamineo jokes with the lawyers: the tragic characters are also capable of comedy. In *The Devil's Law-case* a comic scene again introduces the trial, but it is a scene in which the lawyers jest among themselves and retell unfunny old jokes and Leonora, although present, is almost silent. A comic background is created for near tragic incidents of despair, madness and attempted murder, but the play's two vulnerable and suffering heroines remain wholly serious figures. Comedy is centered on Romelio, but also on more minor and more typical characters, the humorous 'mad' (II.1.198) judge Ariosto, the predatory lawyer Contilupo, the clerk Sanitonella, and the spruce and unprincipled man about town Julio, whose failure to recognise his own father in disguise produces a miniature city comedy. This strategy of directing our comic attention on minor figures is wholly characteristic of the play. Choral figures take on an extraordinary prominence in directing our judgement and in distancing us from the central figures: Ariosto, the Capuchin, Crispiano and the Surgeons all have rôles in the play far more prominent than we might expect from the actions they have to perform. More like *The White Devil* than *The Duchess of Malfi*, the play directs our attention away from individuals and on to a whole society.

On the whole in *The Devil's Law-case* the men, and especially Romelio, represent and support comedy and the women tragedy. The conflict of the sexes and the conflict of the genres are complementary. At one point Romelio disguises himself as a Jewish physician whose accomplishments (III.2.1–16) are modelled on those of Marlowe's Barabas (*The Jew of Malta* II.3.179–203): the gusto with which Romelio adopts this rôle adds a further irony to Marlowe's already ironic and parodic tragedy. Almost every scene in which Romelio meets the women whose lives and passions he so arrogantly tries to control is rich in clashing tones. This is established as early as the second scene of Act One: Romelio tries to compel Jolenta to accept his comic image for her future, an arranged marriage with Ercole, while she insists on tragic images, 'the tomb-maker', 'my coffin' (I.2.2–3).

Act Three Scene Three seems especially central to the establishment of a relationship between the warring genres. Contarino and Ercole have fought a duel over Jolenta: each has seemed to be badly wounded or even to die, but in true tragicomic style each has in fact survived. Romelio in his Jewish disguise has also attempted to kill the badly-wounded Contarino, but ironically enough he instead effects his enemy's recovery. Jolenta, not realising that the man she loves has not been killed, appears with the trappings of tragedy, 'in mourning' for the man she loved with 'two tapers, a death's head, a book' (III.3. initial SD). Romelio jokes flippantly about his affair with the nun Angiolella and feigns to find Jolenta's bitter retort 'pleasant' (III.3.42), while his sister is wrapped in 'sorrow' (III.3.2). Blindly complacent within his own satirical vision, Romelio urges his grief-stricken sister to 'smile' (III.3.157) at the imperfections of life. He also rejects Jolenta's attempt to improvise tragedy by provoking him to kill her with the lie that she is pregnant, a lie which she cynically agrees to assume more permanently by pretending to be the mother of Angiolella's child, thereby saving the reputation of Romelio's mistress the nun. From her tragic view of life Jolenta accepts this comic relief from her own pain, agreeing to pretend pregnancy to 'beguile' her 'sorrow' (III.3.156). However it now seems that comedy is only a mocking device to exacerbate her agony: her genuine sorrow must appear 'fantastical', and must conceal itself behind a surface of comedy, 'a pied fool's coat' (III.3.181–3).

After facing one of the play's representatives of tragedy, Romelio confronts the other. His mother Leonora, ageing and passionate, is drawn with an intensity and simplicity of feeling which approach the tragic, and Romelio's blindness to her pain is as disturbing as his insensitivity to Jolenta's. He continues to 'smile' (III.3.221) at his own lie about Jolenta's pregnancy, while Leonora is horrified, hurt, and 'very sick' (III.3.225) at Romelio's casual admission that he has murdered Contarino. It now seems that comedy is no longer possible. Her love for Contarino was her last chance, her 'last merriment 'fore winter' (III.3.251). Now she devotes herself to tragedy and meditates on revenge. In *The Devil's Law-case* tragedy and comedy clash across the first four acts. Again and again the play exploits ironic divergences between the interpretations of the action made by the various characters. The play sets out to complicate tragicomic and tragic stereotypes and simple genre-definitions as an honest way of depicting its shifting and ambiguous world.

I have already drawn attention to the importance of verbal ambiguities in tragicomedy, of puns, clashing meanings, paradoxes, confusions of literal and metaphorical language, riddles. Plays criticise and deflate the rhetoric of their characters, as the downright Country Fellow mocks Philaster's violent and self-dramatising 'rhetoric' (*Philaster* vol. 1, p. 15), or the conquering king Arbaces is reduced to a grocer returning home with 'peas for all our money' (*A King and No King* II.2.149–50). Semantic misunderstandings are used repeatedly to deflate the pretensions of Beaumont and Fletcher's small tragicomic heroes. Shakespeare's tragicomedies also make much use of riddle and paradox. Pericles must solve a riddle. Mariana's position in *Measure for Measure* can only be expressed in riddling terms:

> I have known my husband; yet my husband
> Knows not that ever he knew me.   (V.1.187–8)

It is Helena in *All's Well that Ends Well*, however, for whom riddles are especially important. She is adept at riddles, which she uses repeatedly and significantly:

> Let us assay our plot; which, if it speed,
> Is wicked meaning in a lawful deed,

> And lawful meaning in a lawful act,
> Where both not sin, and yet a sinful fact.   (III.7.44–7)

Intention and deed, 'meaning' and 'act', are dislocated in the play's tragicomic world. Helena is perhaps so adept at riddles because she feels herself to be the victim of a riddle: in her hopeless love for Bertram, she 'riddle-like, lives sweetly where she dies' (I.3.21). However she is not only a victim and user of riddles. She is also, in the reconciling ending of the play, the embodied solution of the riddles which have disturbed us throughout the play:

> Dead though she be she feels her young one kick.
> So there's my riddle: one that's dead is quick.   (V.3.296–7)

Tragicomedy criticises its own rhetoric and analyses the validity of language by making language play tricks. In *The Devil's Law-case* the case brought by Leonora poses a 'riddle' (IV.2.163) about the identity of Romelio, but this is only one of many riddles, puns, ambiguities and paradoxes in the play.

Although Romelio so convincingly praises 'action' (I.1.55–6), the world at least of the women of the play is one where words have replaced and compromised real action. Leonora admits that she and her waiting woman have spent their lives 'with talking nothing and with doing less' (III.3.375). She has given her servant only 'good words, but no deeds' (III.3.379). Indeed one of the things which Contarino first praises about the older woman is her 'language' (I.1.109). Despite her reliance on words, however, Leonora is particularly apt to misunderstand and misuse them. The whole trail of misunderstandings and recriminations in the play begins because Leonora so entirely misunderstands Contarino's metaphorical request to be given her 'picture' (I.1.135). Contarino is speaking, in metaphor, of Leonora's daughter Jolenta, whom at this point he wishes to marry: Leonora takes him literally and believes he has made a declaration of his love for her.

Leonora's commitment to words prevents her from penetrating beyond the surface of things. One of the most significant emblems associated with her is the picture. Contarino's request for her picture leads her into a lengthy speech about the painting of portraits and the relationship between appearances and the realities they mirror. Her description of the ideal picture in which the 'soul moves in the superficies' (I.1.162–3), though, is an ironic statement of a truth she does not seem to have grasped at a deeper level, that appearances and reality are not necessarily identical. Later Leonora even compares herself with 'one of our best picture-makers' (III.3.252). Her dependence upon language and upon appearances leads her to a lying attempt to discredit her son Romelio by proving him a bastard, but the only case she can make is through lying words and an equally untrustworthy picture. She has kept this portrait of her husband's friend for forty years, but in the trial scene she does not even realise that her judge Crispiano is himself the man in the picture. Nor is she the only person in the play unable to recognise the realities behind appearances. She is precisely parodied in this by Julio, Crispiano's son, who fails to recognise his father in disguise. The play presents us with a world of people who do not recognise the obvious. Leonora is attached to the surface of things, to language rather than action, and she is constantly deceived about the relationship between metaphor and literal truth.

Many other characters in the play are deceived by an ambiguity, riddle, pun or paradox. Leonora fails to realise the metaphorical meaning of Contarino's 'picture' (I.1.135), but other characters are even more seriously confused or mocked by ambiguities. As Romelio prepares to fight a duel with Ercole and the disguised Contarino, whom Romelio still believes he has murdered, the Capuchin, whom Romelio has locked up in a tower, shouts out the crucial information that Contarino is 'living' (V.4.165). Even this clear literal statement, though, is misinterpreted by the devious Romelio:

> Aye, aye, he means he would have Contarino's living
> Bestowed upon his monastery. (V.4.166–7)

Romelio's misinterpretation of language and a too-keen awareness of verbal ambiguity almost lead to disaster. Finally Jolenta writes to Ercole just before the duel, a letter which is both a riddle and a test for her new 'sweetheart' (V.1.28), and which explains her pregnancy:

> She writes back, that the shame she goes withal,
> Was begot by her brother. (V.2.34–5)

Jolenta means that her fictional pregnancy was Romelio's idea: Contarino at least takes her literally and because of his revulsion at the idea of incest any relationship between him and Jolenta becomes impossible. Ambiguity creates musunderstanding and conflict which only just fail to be disastrous in the play's ironic tragicomic world.

The play is very rich in puns, from the most trivial – the lawyer's 'brief' which is anything but 'brief' (IV.1.10–11) – to the most far-reaching – ambiguities about the meanings of words like 'Contarino's living' (V.4.166). The world of the play is deceptive and shifting, and so is its language. Puns, riddles and equivocations demonstrate ways in which language deceives. The play also sets up a system of deflating commentary on the rhetoric of tragedy. Romelio declares his own reckless courage with a conviction worthy of Flamineo or Vittoria:

> Let fear dwell with earthquakes,
> Shipwrecks at sea, or prodigies in heaven;
> I cannot set myself so many fathom
> Beneath the height of my true heart, as fear.   (IV.2.84–7)

The more practical Ariosto, however, immediately mocks and deflates the rhetoric of heroism:

> Very good words, I assure you, if they were
> To any purpose.   (IV.2.88–9)

Words in *The Devil's Law-case* are characteristically equivocal. Not only do they fall easily into double-meanings: it is also difficult, as it is in *A King and No King*, to gauge how permanent is their validity or how real are the effects they create. Perhaps the most important repeated motif which illustrates the equivocal nature of language is the oath or curse. Leonora swears to curse Jolenta should she marry Contarino (I.2.92–5). Later Jolenta, believing Romelio's lying statement that Contarino intended to set up a *ménage à trois* with her and her mother, swears not to marry him (III.2.150–3). Finally Contarino, the third apex of the triangle, is deceived by Jolenta's riddling letter and swears never to marry her (V.2.40). In these three cases words take on a disquieting physical force, creating real and impassible barriers. For partly semantic reasons, the union we expect can never take place. Elsewhere, though, words are 'merely voice' (*A King and No King* IV.4.126) and can easily be revoked and put aside. Angiolella, Leonora and Ercole have all at some time made a monastic vow, but in each case this is easily discarded to allow them to marry. Men and women are too frail to live up to their ideals, and language must reflect this inability. It can function as a kind of action, solid and forceful, or it can function as 'merely voice'. It is impossible to predict and impossible to control.

It is not just that language is unpredictable and ambiguous in *The Devil's Law-case*, however. Although its plot is complex, at each turn it depends on a repeated motif – an action which ironically produces quite a different result from that intended. In the play's last moments the Capuchin points out to us 'how heaven / Can invert man's firmest purpose!' (V.4.193–4): we may doubt the involvement of 'heaven', but the point is otherwise good. Romelio's attempt to murder the dying Contarino not only fails to kill him but actually performs the operation the surgeons had been afraid to attempt and so saves Contarino's life. What Romelio has intended to produce 'an absolute cure' (III.2.107) from life itself turns out to be a 'cure' in simple literal terms. The surgeons draw our attention to the irony involved, 'That his attempt to kill him should become / The very direct way to save his life' (III.2.152–4). This is only the most striking example, though, of a pattern repeated throughout the play. Contarino's laboured attempt to explain himself to Leonora produces only greater mis-understandings. Leonora's law-suit against Romelio recoils against her and discredits her. The final duel leads straight into the happy ending. With so much in the play that is heavily ironic and even fantastic, it is hardly surprising that 'strange' is a key word in the play, actually being used twenty-six times (I.1.14, 195; I.2.174, 222; III.3.203, etc.). Webster frankly accepts the unlikely elements in his plot and makes no attempt to pretend that it is typical. We are looking into a world where 'strange accident' (III.2.147) can undo all plans and intentions, a world where action as well as language can prove ineffective, but where for a moment fate becomes benevolent and all these strange accidents lead, however tentatively, to a happy ending.

Whereas Leonora is associated with the failure of language and the image of painting, Romelio is associated with the failure of action and the image of the play. The Jewish disguise in which he attempts to murder Contarino seems drawn from *The Jew of Malta,* and it is surrounded by images of fiction: 'I could play with my own shadow now' (III.2.2). As we have seen in other tragicomedies, this frank recognition of the play's theatrical nature compromises and undermines its tragic potential. Even in the trial scene, where Romelio is almost the only character not actively engaged in outrageous lies, Contilupo insists on the pretence and unreality associated with Romelio's career. He seems only

A giant in a May-game, that within
Is nothing but a porter. (IV.2.129–30)

The play investigates dilemmas created by the divergence of appearance and reality, of intention and achievement, and two key images of these dichotomies are the picture and the play. Disguises and lies, abrupt changes of mind, verbal double-meanings and broken promises, images of fiction, are all ways in which the tragicomic world defines itself.

Act Five of *The Devil's Law-case* has been given little study as a tragicomic ending. It has been generally felt to be contrived, confused, unconvincing or 'insipid'.[1] Madeleine Doran's account of the play's ending is typical:

> A complicated plot of rivalries in love, duels and disappearances leads up to a fine trial scene in which the conscienceless Leonora's revengeful intentions against her own son are exposed and thwarted. But Webster does not let the findings of the trial govern the outcome of the play. He winds it up with a solution of affairs directly athwart every sympathy he has created, all sense of justice, and what might be called the 'leading' of the plot. Instead of the double ending one expects from such a plot, with the virtuous rewarded and the abductors and traducers at least shamed if not punished, there is an obviously contrived and anticlimactic 'happy' ending. Everyone gets a mate: even Leonora is rewarded with the man she has tried to get away from her own daughter, and the unoffending daughter has her second and less favoured suitor fobbed off on her.[2]

Now it is indisputable that in the final act Webster does contradict the 'leading', or one of the 'leadings', of his plot. We certainly do not expect the virginal heroine to be beaten in the marriage-stakes by her own mother. Northrop Frye has seen in one aspect of comedy a form of the Oedipus conflict, where an old man and a young, often father and son, fight over the same woman.[3] This is very common in Jacobean city comedy, and the young man almost always wins. Webster deliberately varies and inverts this motif by applying it to women, but also by making Leonora and not Jolenta the centre of sympathy. The play suggests conventional genre-structures, but it does so only to break them down, so that Webster deliberately undermines and finally denies the 'leading' of his plot.

The 'leading' of the plot is perhaps not quite as untrustworthy, though, as Miss Doran's account would suggest. Any other relationship, as I have suggested, has been made impossible by the solemn vows of each of the characters involved. Besides, in certain areas of the play small details comically predict the resolution we are given. After the duel which seems so dangerous to both Ercole and Contarino, the body of one of the young men is taken 'to Saint Sebastian's monastery' (II.2.34). St Sebastian, of course, is ironically appropriate here because the saint was wounded with arrows, but according to some accounts did in fact recover. An alert spectator is given the slimmest of clues about the fate of the wounded man. Finally, a number of tiny included tragicomedies also predict the play's ending of averted danger. Jolenta tries, unsuccessfully, to goad Romelio into murdering her, two duels take place in which fatality is avoided. Ironic hints and included tragicomedies predict a tragicomic ending, though at the same time Webster also frustrates some of our expectations in the tragicomic ending we are actually given.

In Fletcher's and Shakespeare's tragicomedy *The Two Noble Kinsmen*, the non-Chaucerian figure of the Gaoler's daughter, pathetically in love with Palamon, seems to be invented solely in order to persuade us that a happy ending is possible, with marriages between her and Palamon, and between Arcite and Emilia: Davenant's adaptation of the play, *The Rivals* (1662), actually uses this happy ending. Much of the power of the original play, however, lies in the abrupt contrast between the happy ending which may seem to be suggested by the 'leading' of the plot and the more ironic and disturbing ending which the play actually gives us. The play ends with marriage but also with death, and with the discovery 'that we should things desire that do cost us / The loss of our desire' (V.4.127–8). Something of the same kind of effect seems to be achieved by Webster's denial of our expectation in *The Devil's Law-case*. Webster certainly hints at a tidy and undisturbing ending. Leonora, the character who really complicates the comic planning, might have been married off to Crispiano: she has kept his picture for forty years, and when she is searching for a fictional lover he is chosen, which might have been used to illustrate some surviving feeling for him. That he is allowed to vanish almost silently suggests a deliberate frustration of our facile romanticising. More in line with Jacobean ideals about widows, Leonora might have withdrawn altogether from the marriage-stakes, like the Queen of Corinth in the tragicomedy of that name by Fletcher and Massinger: again, though, our facile assumptions are attacked, and we are forced to admit that an elderly woman in love has the same rights as her daughter. Finally, although the play itself makes nothing of this, Ercole is described in the introductory list of characters as a Knight of Malta, a member of an order bound by a monastic vow. Like Bertoldo in Massinger's *The Maid of Honour*, Ercole might finally have chosen to respect his order. Webster buries suggestions in the play that these two complicating characters might withdraw to leave the way clear for the juvenile leads. Ercole's name, an Italian version of Hercules, might recall the hero who chose virtue rather than pleasure, and perhaps suggest a similar choice for the play.

However although Webster hints at this undisturbed ending, he packs the play with feeling which works against any such simple conclusion. Bar after bar is placed in the way of the expected ending. Leonora cannot simply deny her own passions, and Crispiano is too shadowy a figure to engage her. Above all, the play repeatedly suggests reservations about the 'great lord' (I.1.26) Contarino as a suitable husband for Jolenta. He doubts her fidelity when she most needs his loving support (I.1.196–8), just as he is suspicious of the honourable Ercole (II.1.286–90). He is wasteful and extravagant (I.2.62–5), thoughtless and unreliable, fighting with Ercole even when he has promised Jolenta not to do so. He uses complex and ambiguous language without realising the problems this can create, as he does when he asks for Leonora's 'picture'. However when this characteristic verbal ambiguity is used against him, he fails to understand it. He lacks the faith in Jolenta to see that her confession that her 'shame' was 'begot by her brother' (V.2.37–8) was not literally true. Ercole on the other hand, as his heroic name would suggest, is generous, tolerant and stable. When he believes Jolenta is pregnant by his rival, he is prepared to marry her in this condition and to be 'honourable' (III.3.314) enough to be a father to her unborn child. The virtuous heroine gets the man who really deserves her: the ageing widow gets the worthless man she so badly wanted. The 'leading of the plot' in the first four acts suggests simple comic and tragic patterns but the play's complex and teasing vision systematically obstructs these patterns and questions their validity. Webster finally refuses to impose the expected patterns on the convincing emotion and vivid uncertainty which the play has created. Its fifth act moves towards a new tragicomic form.

In the play's first four acts both action and language prove to be deceptive, creating grotesque tragicomic ironies. The final act seems particularly intent on weighing up action and language and deciding which is the more trustworthy, and it does this especially by moving from a largely verbal to a largely visual mode. The play up to this point has been full of fictions, verbal, like Leonora's lies or Jolenta's equivocation, or visual, like the disguises adopted by Romelio, Crispiano, Ercole and Contarino. The final act assesses the relationship between the visual and the verbal, and moves the play from its acceptance of fiction to a new grasp of the realities that lie behind appearances.

In Act Five Scene Two the play's growing tendency to replace language by action is especially prominent. The play is becoming increasingly visual: the central conflict is presented primarily in visual terms as Ercole and Contarino enter, 'coming in friars' habits' (V.2.13 SD). This visual centre introduces and contrasts with Jolenta's equivocating letter, one of the play's most potent images of the ways in which language deceives. Contarino, so adept himself at using ambiguous language, fails to understand the real meaning of Jolenta's letter. He even remains in disguise now that there seems no adequate reason to do so. He asks himself why he does so (V.2.15–20), but provides no satisfactory answer: he simply thrives on concealing himself behind metaphor, unwilling to face literal truth. Like Leonora, he is devoted to appearances rather than reality, and their eventual union is consequently perhaps not as strange as it appears.

Act Five Scene Three again presents clashing genre definitions and takes important steps away from fiction and towards the revelation of the truth. The Surgeon, now Winifred's admirer, reveals to her the truth about Contarino. This revelation, however, cannot be made simply, but in this complex tragicomic world requires a whole mass of images of fiction, and theatricality to express itself convincingly. In order to reveal the truth the Surgeon must take on Romelio's abandoned Jewish disguise. The genres continue to clash. Like a tragic heroine, Jolenta seems 'a little mad' (V.3.29), but it is promised that the revelation of the 'comical event' (V.3.29) will restore her sanity. Comedy and tragedy collide, and paradoxically it seems that truth can only be told by means of an elaborate fiction.

Act Five Scene Four begins in an aimless, low-pitched comic scene which is cut across by the entrance of Romelio, 'very melancholy' (V.4.39 SD). The Capuchin tries to compel him to adopt a Christian, and in this context that seems to mean a tragic, view of life, to 'meditate of death' (V.4.54). Romelio refuses to respond. He would rather 'laugh' (V.4.63), and he adopts the cool bravado of a Flamineo: 'I will be mine own pilot' (V.4.52). Yet again Romelio's tragic rhetoric is undermined and we are detached from it. At the same time it is hardly possible, though, to accept the Capuchin as an ideal figure and a serious spokesman for absolute values. The play has already suggested strong reservations about those dedicated to the monastic life. Angiolella and perhaps Ercole have broken monastic vows, and

Leonora's view of the Capuchin's order is punningly cynical:

> For indeed mischiefs are like the visits
> Of Franciscan friars, they never come
> To prey upon us single.   (III.3.205–7)

In the final act the Capuchin is made to look ridiculous as he is locked in a tower with Leonora, and as Julio makes cynical remarks about his relationship with the older woman. Romelio's half-parodic Websterian bravado and the Capuchin's solid Christian assumptions are both ironically undercut. Simple viewpoints seem always unacceptable in Webster's complex and relativistic tragicomic world.

Up to now the scene's effects have been largely verbal ones as Romelio and the Capuchin present their strikingly different views of the situation. Again the scene is cut across by another visual passage, a 'dumb pageant' (V.4.130) in which Leonora enters, 'with two coffins borne by her servants, and two winding sheets stuck with flowers, presents one to her son, and the other to Julio' (V.4.109 SD). Leonora, who has trusted so unwisely in words, now tries to express her pain visually and in terms of objects. Tragedy and the threat of tragedy are distanced by being presented so exclusively in visual, and in musical, terms.

This 'pageant' with its striking and disturbing iconography and its avoidance of the ambiguity with which language now seems inevitably invested might have precipitated tragic 'knowledge' and the telling of the truth. Romelio, though, simply retreats into another fiction, a claim to penitence which only allows him to conceal his real intentions. After Leonora's 'pageant' with its suggestions of tragedy, the Capuchin tries, like the Duke in *Measure for Measure*, to reassert comfortably and easily the tragicomic form:

> And now that I have made you fit for death,
> And brought you even as low as is the grave,
> I will raise you up again . . .
> . . . turn this intended duel
> To a triumph.   (V.4.143–7)

However, as is appropriate for a play where every intention goes ironically wrong, this attempt to make heavenly comforts of despair also, for the moment, fails. The Capuchin, would-be stage-manager of the tragicomic revelation, is humiliatingly locked up with Leonora in a tower, while Julio makes snide remarks about the young Capuchin's relationship with the older woman.

The final scene of the play opens on this world of inverted intentions and misunderstood words. To an increasing extent the play is expressing its dilemmas visually, in terms of spectacle and emblematic objects, rather than verbally. Throughout the last act we as audience are placed very much on the outside of the action, observing its pageantry and its visual, unverbal precision: the language of the duel even moves briefly from English into French. Romelio, however, suddenly cuts across these rigid ceremonial forms: 'Stay, I do not well know whither I am going' (V.6.9). The machiavel's trust in action collapses, and he now tries not to replace self-glorifying action with Christian consolation, but rather to have both at once. The Capuchin is sent for, but the duel still continues. Romelio's hesitation here has been seen as a result of the workings of divine grace, perhaps 'unconvincing', but nevertheless 'a miracle'.[4] Webster, though, carefully understates a providential interpretation. This is simply another example of those abrupt tragicomic reversals in which the play is so rich, another intention producing an ironically inappropriate result. Webster's view of this central malcontent-manipulator figure has anyway changed significantly in the course of his writing career. Flamineo on the whole tells us the truth about the dark and dangerous world of his play, where Bosola's view of the world is questioned and undercut. Romelio is even less reliable a commentator: he is satirised as well as satirist, and as the play goes on we become increasingly distanced from him. Romelio the actor finally distrusts the action which gave him power. In a deliberate tragicomic strategy, the final scene gives increasingly incomplete explanations of the behaviour and feelings of the people in the play. The central figures Romelio and Leonora now have very little left to say in the play, and it falls apart into spectacle, short speeches and sketchy explanations, detaching us from the fiction and confronting us unavoidably with its theatrical nature.

Because of Romelio's sudden distrust of action the happy ending becomes possible. In a final tragicomic discord, the duel is again interrupted by the entrance of Leonora with her good news. Previously a supporter of tragedy, Leonora now appears on the side of comedy, reconciliation and renewal. The statement that 'Contarino's living' (V.6.21) which Romelio had previously misinterpreted is now revealed as a simple literal truth as Contarino finally casts off his disguise. Metaphor gives way to literal truth, fiction to fact, and the audience is prepared for the ending of the fiction which is the play.

Madeleine Doran found that the ending contradicted the 'leading' of the plot in the way that Leonora is finally accepted as a wife by Contarino, the accepted lover of her daughter.[5] Lucas found it difficult to determine even what is happening here,[6] and the whole startling shift is dealt with in three lines of dialogue (V.6.24–6). This seems not to be a lack of clarity, however, but yet another example of the play's growing tendency to explain to the eye rather than to the ear: the shift in relationships is expressed in visual patterning rather than in language, and in performance would be perfectly clear. Action and language are becoming ever more separate: the complex riddling language of the first encounter of Leonora and Contarino has been replaced by almost no language at all. However although the process of staging would dispose of some of the problems implicit in this ending, this new relationship remains an equivocal one. Leonora suddenly 'claims to be nearer' (V.6.25) to Contarino than a casual friend and he steps into the place of her recognised lover, having now 'vowed' (V.6.26) his life to her. In a society which treats oaths both so lightly and so seriously this vow inevitably has an ambiguous status, and we are disturbingly reminded of all the broken vows in the play. The newly formed relationships are surrounded by question marks: Contarino has spent much of the play flattering the older woman to her face and insulting her behind her back, and Romelio's slanderous suggestion that Contarino loves Leonora only 'for her money' (III.3.136) is never contradicted. In this relationship at least the play's ending gives a sceptical redefinition of comedy, making the relationship so abrupt, so lacking in verbal explanation, and so rooted in fiction and pretence. However it is a happy ending of sorts, and even Romelio accepts the values of comedy: 'If I do not / Dream, I am happy too' (V.6.26–7).

The play, then, is now explaining and resolving its changing relationships far less in verbal terms than in terms of pageantry, spectacle, and stage patterning. The most elaborate piece of visual explanation still remains. A procession enters, 'Angiolella veiled and Jolenta, her face coloured like a Moor, the two surgeons, one of them like a Jew' (V.6.28 SD). Ercole and Contarino resolve their own confusions by adopting disguise: so does Jolenta. This Moor-disguise and the pageant which contains it even repeat quite precisely some of the play's already established images of fiction, providing that double-vision so characteristic of tragicomedy. Leonora entered the trial scene to erect an impressive structure of fiction 'with a black veil over her' (IV.2.43 SD): now Angiolella is veiled. Ercole and Contarino prepared to fight the duel dressed 'in friars' habits' (V.2.13 SD): now Angiolella and Jolenta are dressed as nuns. Romelio now that he has abandoned acting and disguise finds himself facing his own Jewish disguise on one of the surgeons: the disguise in which he attempted murder is now re-used to bring the good news of the comic conclusion. It is a scene of mirror-images and of purely visual links between characters, a rather, indeed, Pirandellian conclusion. In the final scene of *Enrico IV* the central character, now recovered from the delusion that he is Henry IV, faces an actor playing his own younger self, and the Marquesa and her daughter, each dressed as Matilda, also confront each other. Past and present, fact and fiction, are juxtaposed in visual terms, and are first confused and then sharply differentiated in much the same way as in *The Devil's Law-case*. In Webster's play, however, this repetition and the accumulation of mirror-images leads not to disaster but to the play's rather solemn happy ending. Jolenta's pageant recalls visually earlier images of hostility and disharmony which are now to be dismissed, and the happy ending is predicted by her own tacit willingness to accept a second-best rôle in the changing society.

Jolenta has seemed a passive pawn in the game for most of the play. Now, like Romelio in his attempt to murder Contarino and Leonora in her law-suit, she takes action into her own hands, and like them she does so through disguise and pretence. Disguise is not inevitably threatening. After all, it is the principle by which the play operates and can also be benevolent and reconciling.

The Moor-disguise in part simply heralds the happy ending and predicts festivity: it was so common a feature of the iconography of the Elizabethan masque that this general suggestion seems an inevitable part of its significance.[7] More specifically, it is also an emblem for Jolenta's 'blackened' reputation, and it is a visual riddle which becomes a test for Ercole, her current 'sweetheart' (V.1.28), and also for the audience, who must also not be deceived by her 'blackened' appearance. Contarino has failed her tests: he has mistrusted her, misunderstood her, lied to her, and finally left her for her own mother. At this point in the scene it is even harder to assess the state of the relationship between Ercole and Jolenta than it is that between Contarino and Leonora: it is even more abruptly understated. Ercole simply has a line and a half (V.6.50–1) to ask Jolenta to explain her behaviour. There is no longer any discussion of their feelings, commitment to each other, or plans for the future: Ercole by asking this question has simply become the person in the scene with most interest in Jolenta.

Contarino has failed Jolenta's tests. It is Ercole who passes the test implied by the pageant by refusing to judge Jolenta only by her blackened appearance, and who responds to her insistence that he must look below the surface:

> Like or dislike me, choose you whether: . . .
> Hence vain show! I only care
> To preserve my soul most fair.   (V.6.34–9)

However he passes the test negatively rather than positively: he does not misjudge Jolenta, but we are given little help in assessing the quality of his feelings for her. Like Bassanio in *The Merchant of Venice*, Ercole is asked to choose between appearances and reality, and must bring about the happy ending by rejecting 'vain show' (V.6.38). Bassanio has a long and elaborate meditation pointing out to us very clearly the moral basis of his action (*Merchant* III.2.73–107). Ercole has no such thing: he has only a line and a half to speak in the play that remains, and that is only to ask Jolenta why she has disguised herself, and that receives only a partial and evasive answer. The relationship between Jolenta and Ercole is established and consolidated by words hardly at all, but only by stage patterning. In the last scene of *Measure for Measure* Shakespeare has Isabella make no verbal response to the Duke's repeated proposal of marriage: less confident than comedy, this play surrounds the comic relationships of love and marriage with uneasy silences or even protests. Similarly Webster gives us the comic pattern but not the wholeheartedness of comedy, and his omissions and silences draw our attention to the convincing imperfection of these new relationships.

The Devil's Law-case engages in an experiment to find out how much of the work of drama can be done in visual terms, and what cannot be done in this way remains undone. Leonora presents a letter which will clarify the extraordinary action, a final device which seems to mock the power of language. Romelio agrees to marry Angiolella and make restitution, Angiolella gives some practical advice to 'honest virgins' (V.6.78). It seems as if the actors are already stepping out of their rôles, shedding their fictional individuality as a preparation for the end of the play. The central place is taken not by those so painfully involved in the events of the play but by the detached commentator

Ariosto, who sums up the precariousness of the comic ending with its 'rareness and difficulty' (V.6.59), and allots appropriate punishments, mostly token ones.

However one important effect remains, Ariosto's final definition of the genre of the play. He insists, like the Surgeon earlier (V.3.29), that what we have seen is only 'these so comical events' (V.6.62). Romelio accedes to this: he is 'happy too' (V.6.27), and 'most willingly' (V.6.75) agrees to marry his pregnant mistress the nun. Finally Julio plans to go to sea 'with a rare consort / Of music' (V.6.70–1). In the last scene the insistence upon comedy and reconciliation, masque and music, collides with the deliberate and understated dubiousness of the reforming relationships. As in the last scene of *Measure for Measure*, silence attacks the rather strident insistence upon comedy and leaves us disturbed and uncertain. The comic form remains, but it is extended by these tragicomic discords, creating an honest sense of the precariousness and 'difficulty' (V.6.59) of comedy which only increases its poignancy.

Webster's introductory letter to *The Devil's Law-case* points out that 'A great part of the grace of this . . . lay in action' (13–14). This is not only a generous tribute to his actors, but also a statement about the nature of his play. In a precise way performance is especially important in *The Devil's Law-case*, where the very process of enactment does not only clarify but actually creates plot and relationships. Usually a very verbal playwright, Webster experiments in the final act to discover whether simple spectacle can be less ambiguous than language, which the people in the play have found so deceptive. The act is packed with spectacular visual images, the duel, the disguises used by Contarino and Ercole, Leonora's 'dumb pageant' (V.4.130), the Surgeon's use of Romelio's cast-off Jewish costume, Jolenta's disguise as a nun and a moor. In the final scenes of *The White Devil* and *The Duchess of Malfi*, Webster ironically and significantly recalls the past by repeated words and images. Here in *The Devil's Law-case* this is done not verbally but visually. The last act sets up resonant mirror-images, recalling the past and promising a happy, if rather subdued, ending.

'Grace . . . in action' is also peculiarly important because *The Devil's Law-case* is, among other things, also a play about plays and an analysis of theatricality. The play holds up against each other the two instruments of drama, language and spectacle, to discover whether one is more trustworthy or more conclusive than the other. The play begins in a largely verbal mode, but as it goes on spectacle replaces the ambiguities of language with its mute solidity. As I have suggested, the whole play is rich in play-images and play quotations and of tiny included dramas, and nowhere is this more important than in the final scene. The play even investigates its own 'comical' identity (V.3.29, V.6.62), an insistence tinged with irony, so that we are forced to examine the significance of a 'comical' ending which is nevertheless so reticent and imperfect.

Most of the tragicomedies I have considered up to now end with a conscious banishment of fiction and a return to real life. *The Tempest* moves from the magic island to the 'bare island' (Ep.8) of the stage, the fiction of *The Malcontent* crumbles as 'the rest of idle actors idly part' (V.4.194). Even in a Fletcherian tragicomedy like *A King and No King* the final surprise dislocates our involvement with the play and detaches us from the fiction which is approaching its end. In the last act of *The Devil's Law-case* small included dramas draw our attention to the fictional nature of the play, and the rejection of 'vain show' (V.6.38) is at least in part a banishment of the fictional form of the play. It is not just, though, that these enactments mediate for the audience between the fictional world and the real world to which we are about to return. Language, always ambiguous, now becomes increasingly unimportant and perfunctory, and also marks our growing detachment from the characters of the play and from their world. The play turns away from individuals, even from the convincing and compelling dilemmas of Leonora, Romelio and Jolenta: we are increasingly looking not at characters but through them at the fabric of the play. *The Devil's Law-case* is not a failed tragedy that goes to pieces in the last act, but a successful play in a different mode, a critical and analytic tragicomedy with a strong theatrical self-consciousness. What we finally remember about the play is not only Romelio's bravado, or the pain of Leonora, or the characteristically vivid Websterian verse and imagery, but also an exploration which moves out from individuals to wider dilemmas concerning the nature of life, of language, and of drama.

'Riddles and paradoxes':
tragicomedy in
A Cure for a Cuckold

John Webster began and ended his career as playwright with plays written in collaboration. *A Cure for a Cuckold* (1625) is the latest play in which his hand can be seen with any certainty. There seems no reason to doubt the attribution of the play to Webster and William Rowley made by Francis Kirkman, the bookseller who was responsible for the play's first publication in 1661. In some areas of the play, and especially in the tragicomic plot, 'Webster's constructional rhythm'[1] appears clearly, while others, particularly the Compass plot, show Rowley's tricks of style: his characteristic contractions, his love of puns and grammatical jokes, a characteristic linking of speeches by words carried over from one to another, a tendency to drop a syllable out of a line of verse to be replaced by a significant gesture, sigh, or pause.[2] Some critics have also wanted to assign a part in the play to Thomas Heywood:[3] evidence here seems very slight, and a significant number of parallels between *A Cure* and the works of Heywood turn out to come from *Fortune by Land and Sea*, a play on which Rowley also collaborated. It may even be that Rowley is gently parodying his old collaborator in some comic touches: the name of the father of Urse Compass's bastard in *A Cure*, Frankford, is also the name of the virtuous Christian husband in Heywood's *A Woman Killed with Kindness* (1603).

William Rowley (?1585–1626) was an actor as well as a dramatist, and he brought to his writing a practical knowledge of the resources of his theatre and of his actors and an understanding of the tastes of his audience. A prolific playwright, he began writing in about 1607, but his heyday was between 1617 and 1626, when he was often writing two or three plays a year. His independent plays, city comedies, middle-class heroic plays or tragedies of sex and blood are lively, varied and individual, but they are often crude and characters and situations are often repeated from play to play. However although he was not a great playwright on his own account, he also had a genius for collaboration, for bringing out the best in his collaborator and for helping to produce plays which are ordered and coherent despite their joint authorship. In his busy career he collaborated with Day, Wilkins, Heywood, Massinger, Dekker, Fletcher, Ford and Webster, and especially with Thomas Middleton. His collaboration with Middleton was a rich and long-lasting one: it produced, among other plays, one of Middleton's most successful tragicomedies, *A Fair Quarrel* (1617), and what is perhaps Middleton's greatest tragedy, *The Changeling* (1622). It is traditional to regard Rowley as a hack, but his involvement in so many successful plays rather suggests a practical man of the theatre with a keen eye for popular taste and a fruitful ability to organise collaborative plays into coherent structures. Webster and Rowley were friends at least as early as 1623, when Rowley contributed verses in commendation of *The Duchess of Malfi* 'To his friend John Webster'. In 1624 the two had collaborated with Dekker and Ford on *The Late Murder in Whitechapel, or Keep the Widow Waking*, a double-plot play based on two contemporary scandals, apparently with one comic and one tragic plot.[4] On the basis of this exercise in collaboration, they seem to have decided to co-operate again on *A Cure for a Cuckold*, a play which was to be among the last works, if it is not the last work, of each writer.

Where *The Devil's Law-case* shows tragicomedy at its darkest, *A Cure for a Cuckold* is strongly slanted towards comedy. It uses laughter less extensively than any of Webster's independent plays: because of its more simply comic tone and structure, it does not need to define its comic nature as stridently or as ironically as *The Devil's Law-case*. Still, comedy does not go unchallenged. Words and gestures that might suggest comedy tend to be subdued – smiles rather than laughter, 'merry' rather than 'comical' – and they are often subdued even further by a tendency to place them in a context which undermines or contradicts them, compares them with sadness, or uses them ironically or aggressively. This is especially true at the beginning of the play, but the juxtaposition of comedy with sadness or danger is an important part of the effect throughout. In the first scene Lessingham responds to the 'mirth' (I.1.5) of the wedding day, but this is immediately contrasted with Clare's 'sad' state (I.1.23). In the second scene Lessingham is described as one who 'was wont to be compos'd of mirth' (I.2.32), but he too is now sad. Finally in the last scene Woodruff unsuccessfully tries to moderate Bonvile's anger against Annabel by laughing (V.1.237) and by describing the situation 'in laughter' (V.1.235), but these are undermined by the disturbing violence of this scene.

A Cure, then, has a secure comic identity but undermines this by ironic contrasts and by a subdued use of the language of comedy. Comedy is further tested, too, by the play's view of society and personal relationships in the early scenes. As we expect of comedy, the play moves towards a consolidation of personal relationships: Compass and Urse, Annabel and Bonvile, Lessingham and Clare, Bonvile and Woodruff and Rochfield, all move from dissension or infidelity to reconciliation. In the early part of the play, though, all relationships seem menaced or inadequate: Frankford is unfaithful to his wife Luce, Urse Compass is unfaithful to her husband, Clare disrupts Lessingham's friendship for Bonvile and seems set also to break up the relationship between Bonvile and Annabel, and she fights with and refuses Lessingham who loves her. Even Rochfield seems betrayed by his family, who have produced children without the money to support them as gentlemen. None of this dissension or misfortune, however, is permanent, and the sophisticated Caroline society moves clearly along the comic path from disorder to reconciliation. At the same time comedy is modified by the convincing violence of its disorder.

Perhaps because of its collaborative origins, *A Cure* has a multiple plot structure. In the tragicomic plot, in which Webster's hand is most obvious, the wedding celebrations of Bonvile and Annabel are interrupted by the bickering of Clare and Lessingham. Clare sets a horrifying condition which Lessingham must meet if he is to gain her love: he must kill his best friend. Testing his friends, Lessingham finds that only the newly-married Bonvile is sincere and unselfish in his friendship, and he persuades Bonvile to leave his new wife and go with him to Calais, ostensibly as a second in a duel. At Calais, Lessingham reveals that his enemy is Bonvile himself. Bonvile insists that Lessingham has fulfilled Clare's condition and killed his friend by killing Bonvile's friendship for him, and the two return home alive and well. Here more bickering and misunderstanding takes place among the four young people, but eventually all are reconciled. In the comic plot, where Rowley's hand seems most obvious, Compass the sailor returns home to find that his wife has had a bastard in his absence. He not only forgives her but accepts her child with enthusiasm, even winning him legally from his natural father. Compass and his erring wife then quickly divorce and remarry as a stratagem for curing his cuckoldry. Between these two plots is a slighter plot in which the poverty-stricken younger son Rochfield determines to become a thief, but he is helped by Annabel and instead turns out to be a Heywoodian middle-class hero. The play includes material of strikingly different kinds, and what is most surprising is how completely the authors draw this material into a coherent structure.

It is characteristic of Rowley's collaborative plays to have a multiple plot structure, but a structure in which the multiple plots are clearly linked by key words, by repeated situations or parallel characters. In *A Fair Quarrel*, a play which is quoted in *A Cure*, the central duel between Captain Ager and the Colonel is parodied in the subplot, where Chough and Trimtram study at a school of roaring. The serious duel is precipitated because the passionate Colonel insults Ager's mother by calling him 'the son of a whore' (I.1.346). In the comic plot the bouts of roaring also include outrageous insults: 'Thy mother is a calicut, a panagron, a duplar, and a sindicus' (IV.1.110–11). The subplot parodies the intensity of the tragicomic plot and places it in a wider context. Again, *The Changeling* also has a double-plot structure. Isabella, who is morally sane in a mad world, is a counterbalance for Beatrice-Joanna who, as her schizophrenic name suggests,[5] is morally far more ambiguous. Deflores, hired by Beatrice-Joanna to murder the fiancé she no longer loves so that she can marry Alsemero, insists to Beatrice's horror that his fee is her own person. He tries to kiss her as a sign that she now belongs to him (III.3.90). This taut tragic scene, however, gains a new significance in context. It directly follows a scene of the comic subplot, where the lecherous old Lollio tries to kiss the virtuous Isabella (III.2.215), and she threatens to have him murdered by one of her disguised suitors if he persists. In *The Changeling* the plots are linked not only by parallel incidents and characters: key words also link the plots, words like 'change' (V.199–214), 'labyrinth' (III.3.72: IV.3.101), 'hell' and the game of barley-break (III.2.151: V.3.165), for instance. Tragedy or potential tragedy is placed in a larger context, and the very different parts of the play are organised into a coherent whole.

Like *The Changeling* and *A Fair Quarrel*, *A Cure for a Cuckold* is a coherent whole where scenes and plots are linked by repeated words, images and situations. The plots are carefully used to cast significant light on each other. The two most developed plots, although linked only indirectly – Frankford the father of Mrs Compass's child is Annabel's uncle and a guest at her wedding – are closely related in theme and language. Compass the cured cuckold is more than a character in the subplot, but is a central figure who provides a background of values more secure and sympathetic than those of the tragicomic plot. In the main plot the young people mistrust each other, bicker and equivocate, and launch violent attacks on each other verbally or physically. In the subplot Compass forgives his erring wife and no obstacle to their happiness can stand before his grasp of comedy and his good humour. The effect of this plot is to rebuke the excesses of the tragicomic characters and to expose their blatant theatricality. A representative of the all-powerful and all-tolerant comic spirit, Compass has such secure comic control over his own plot that it even extends outward into the tragicomic plot. Not only does he persuade the quarrelling lawyers that he is the lawful father of Frankford's natural child: in an almost magical sense it also seems that his final entrance brings about the happy ending as the young men hear his wedding music and become reconciled. He meets the tragicomic heroes for the first time in this final scene, having existed throughout the play as a contrast for them, and his curing presence gives us confidence in their happy ending. As the background of madmen in *The Changeling* comments on Beatrice-Joanna's moral insanity, so the Compass plot provides a norm of sanity and moderation for the irrational passions of tragicomedy.

The two plots are more precisely linked by the repetition of significant words. The word 'compass' especially is repeated as a link between plots. As the name of the central character of the comic plot it is richly ambiguous. Compass is a sailor and so has the name of a piece of nautical equipment. More to the point, it is a piece of equipment designed to help us find our direction, which is Compass's task in the play. The lost way and the loss of direction are repeated motifs in the play, and a compass is obviously to be useful here. Compass also means, of course, 'measure: proper proportion' (*SOED*), and again Compass's rôle in the play is to assert this. Finally another possible seventeenth-century meaning would be 'artifice, ingenuity ... cunning' (*SOED*): again a suitable name for the man who implements the device for curing cuckoldry.

The repeated use of the word 'compass' keeps the hero of the comic plot firmly in our minds even at the tautest moments of the tragicomic plot. At the end of the first scene the wedding festivities of Annabel and Bonvile have been undermined by the passionate quarrel between Lessingham and Clare. Luce Frankford comments on another imperfect love-relationship, her own with her adulterous husband, who has fathered a child on Urse Compass. Luce puns obscenely on the paradox that her husband has been unfaithful, and yet has at the same time kept himself 'within compass' (I.1.201). More seriously, the word recurs at one of the play's most highly charged moments. When Bonvile has gone to Calais with Lessingham to fight, Annabel is hurt and puzzled by the mysterious disappearance of her husband. She is in a painfully equivocal position, a

> Miserable creature! a Maid, a Wife,
> And Widow in the Compass of two days.   (III.3.23–4)

The pain and danger of the extreme tragicomic dilemma is modified by this ironic reminder of the security of the comic subplot. Finally after the fiasco in Calais, Bonvile praises Lessingham to Clare as one who has always behaved nobly, 'led by the Compass of a noble heart' (IV.2.201): again a reminder of the comic plot modifies and undercuts the violence and vindictiveness of tragicomedy.

Another motif which links the plots is the characteristically Websterian one of the lost way. In the tragicomic plot especially characters repeatedly express their sense of disorientation and doubt in this clear image. At the beginning of the play Lessingham feels that he is 'in a labyrinth' (I.1.68). Annabel had lost her way (II.4.86) when she met the thief Rochfield, and by a comic inversion it is she who must take the thief's arm and 'guide' (II.2.109) him home. Bonvile is 'lost' to Lessingham (III.1.134), Annabel fears that she will lose her husband and be 'lost, lost ... for ever' (III.3.12), and Clare feels that Lessingham has misunderstood her so completely that she too is 'lost for ever' (IV.2.36). In striking contrast, Compass comes back apparently from the dead, and is not 'one that's lost' (II.4.25), but rather 'one that's found again' (II.4.26). Because of this he can, by his simple presence, show the road to the tragicomic characters. With the help of this 'compass' Clare, herself one of the 'lost' (IV.2.36) people in the early part of the play, can become the 'clew' (V.1.348) to lead her friends out of 'this labyrinth' (V.1.349).

Other words and images unite the plots in a rather slighter way. Rochfield is literally a thief: Lessingham has metaphorically 'stolen time' (I.1.41) and 'robbed himself' (I.1.42) to win Clare. More important are repeated images of education and of immaturity: a central theme of the play is the education of the young people in making secure and unselfish relationships. Clare and Lessingham have been 'truants in Love's school' (I.1.19), but Clare wishes never 'to become graduate' (I.1.22) in the study of love. Rochfield is 'but a freshman' (II.2.42) in the art of theft, 'a young physician' (II.2.52) who needs a co-operative patient. Annabel is 'so young and ignorant a scholar' (II.1.30) in love that she does not know how to react when her husband leaves her on her wedding day. Compass, although he does not need this sort of education, is 'new born' (II.3.90) into the world, and is associated throughout the play with children, real and metaphorical.

The play, then, gains coherence from repeated words, 'compass' and 'lost' for instance, and from images of theft, education and children. Another important point is that each plot deals with a similar motif. Each turns on a paradox, and the main characters of each plot are placed in a paradoxical position. Rochfield is 'an honest thief' (II.2.8). Compass is simultaneously a father and not a father, a cuckold and not a cuckold, a widower but also a married man. Urse too is simultaneously wife and widow, and their 'divorce' (IV.1.214) actually marks their reconciliation. In the tragicomic plot Lessingham both has and has not killed his friend Bonvile. Annabel is both wife and virgin (II.2.18) and perhaps, she fears, widow.

Paradox also spills over into the play's ironic inversion of genres. The comic subplot of cuckoldry turns out to be more genuinely concerned with love and understanding than the tragicomic plot with its violence and selfishness: it is the comic hero and not the tragicomic hero who points out the right way to live in society comfortably and forgivingly. Of the play's many 'Riddles and Paradoxes' (I.2.46) only Compass is securely in control. He uses the paradox of divorce leading to reconcilement, and he commits a metaphorical suicide which actually leads to the happy ending. Bonvile like Compass devises a metaphorical death when he insists that Lessingham has killed his friend by killing his friendship, but he handles the paradox far less securely and constructively than Compass. The play depends on Compass to show ways of using the paradoxical situation positively and as a way of reaching the happy ending.

Tragicomic discords are created in the play not only between the contrasting plots. Clashing tones even exist in the Compass plot, which is so solidly comic in its control and its honest acceptance of imperfection. When he has just returned to Blackwall, Compass talks about children conceived out of wedlock and about barren marriages, and the two boys sympathetically find this 'horrible' (II.3.48) and 'pitiful' (II.3.52), hinting at the reactions of tragedy. However Compass's security defeats these suggestions and creates a moving climate of restrained emotions, allowing him to be 'merry' (II.3.112, 113) even when he learns about his wife's illegitimate child.

Moreover Compass attracts some resonant imagery which even suggests Shakespearean romance. He goes through the fundamental romance process, through death to rebirth, not once but twice. He reappears at Blackwall, having been given up for dead: 'I heard thou wert dived to the bottom of the sea . . . / Never to come to Blackwall again' (II.3.93–5). However he is not dead but reborn: 'I am new come into the world, and children cry before they laugh' (II.3.88–9). Later in the play he enacts a metaphorical death – 'I will go hang myself two hours' (IV.1.221) – before being reborn to remarry Urse and accept her illegitimate child. In other ways too Compass's position reminds us of some characters of Shakespearean romance. He is a sailor and like Pericles or Prospero he is surrounded by marine imagery. As in *Pericles* or *The Tempest* the sea is threatening but also saving: Urse is to 'drown' (IV.1.221) herself metaphorically in order to achieve her happy ending. Like Marina or Perdita, Compass is finally reunited with his family, one who 'was lost', but is now 'found again' (II.4.25–7). Finally like Leontes or Pericles he finally rediscovers his lost child, though in a very different way from these two heroes. The Compass plot is rich and moving in its varied tones, not only of city comedy but also of romance, and with the faintest hint of more disturbing emotions behind them, but for once these are easily resisted and controlled.

In the tragicomic plot rapid and vertiginous changes of tone are even more important a part of the effect. The play opens on a wedding festivity, 'feasting and . . . joy . . . triumphs and ovations' (I.1.1–2). Festivity, however, is immediately attacked by the violence and selfishness of Clare and Lessingham. In an entirely egocentric attempt to claim that he has bought Clare with his 'services' (I.1.49), Lessingham sees Bonvile's wedding-day as a time of 'mirth' (I.1.5). Clare sulkily insists that she is not capable of being 'merry' (I.1.103). The play opens with these collisions of tone: it begins as it ends with comic motif of marriage and music, but comedy is immediately qualified by Clare's curt refusal to join it and by Lessingham's narrow self-centredness. The multiple vision of the play, its deflation of the dignity of tragedy and the highly charged emotionalism of tragicomedy, begins in this scene of clashing 'mirth' and 'melancholy'.

Lessingham with his aggressive egocentricity and Clare with her painful sense of disorientation, are obviously equivocal characters, but the play's ironic vision extends even to those characters who seem less ambiguous. The virtuous Annabel, perfect woman and wife, turns briefly into a fish-wife in the last act. Conventions according to which the hero behaves with total self-sacrifice are also treated ironically. Bonvile's very name suggests his goodness, and he generously leaves his marriage unconsummated and risks his life in order to help his friend. Even this show of magnanimity, though, is gently discredited:

> I still prefer my friend before my pleasure,
> Which is not lost for ever – but adjourned
> For more mature employment.   (I.2.183–5)

The heroic disinterest in the first line is immediately qualified. Bonvile's uneasy compromise between romance and realism only makes him look slightly ridiculous.

The multiple plots of *A Cure for a Cuckold* are therefore linked by clashing tones and by repeated words, images and themes. As is characteristic of tragicomedy the plots are also linked by the ambiguity of their language and the difficulty of distinguishing between literal and metaphorical usages. The play asks us to think again about the meanings of perfectly ordinary words like 'father' and 'friend'. Frankford is literally the father of Urse's child, but the play insists that Compass, with his genuine and direct expressions of feeling, is the symbolic father. Whole situations are created and destroyed semantically. Bonvile completely changes Clare's love for him simply by using the word 'whore' (IV.2.214): we are reminded of the climax of *The Changeling*, where Alsemero's accusation that his wife is a whore precipitates the tragic ending, and 'blasts a beauty to deformity' (V.3.32). Compass's comic power is also indicated by his power over language. His control of metaphor convinces the lawyers and even Frankford that the child belongs to its mother, and his vital imagery of boars and sows defeats Frankford's rather sterile images of commerce, law and money. Even in the final scene, Compass playfully uses riddles and paradoxes. In a play where metaphor and the misunderstanding of metaphor can appear so threatening, Compass is the one character who infallibly uses metaphor to produce the happy ending.

Compass uses metaphor and enacted fiction as part of his firm comic control, but in the main plot metaphor is more difficult to identify and to use. Bonvile's metaphorical death lacks the good-humoured comedy of Compass's. Lessingham has 'slain his friend' (III.1.141, 143) by destroying not Bonvile but Bonvile's friendship for him. And Bonvile takes this quibble a stage further by refusing to sail back to England with his ex-friend because "Tis dangerous living / At sea, with a dead body' (III.1.167–8). Metaphor here remains disturbingly violent, where Compass's leads directly to the happy ending.

The most striking example in the play of the ambiguous power of language is Clare's command to Lessingham:

> Prove all thy friends, find out the best and nearest,
> Kill for my sake that friend that loves thee dearest.   (I.1.118–19)

A similar situation occurs in at least two other tragicomedies of the period. In Marston's *The Dutch Courtesan* (1604), Franceschina promises herself to Malheureux if he will kill her ex-lover Frevil, who has abandoned her and whom she now hates. Malheureux however reveals his situation to Frevil, and the two men stage an elaborate pretence of quarrel and murder. In *The Parliament of Love* (1624), on which Rowley may have collaborated with Massinger, Leonora, whose impatient lover Claremond has tried to rape her, seeks to revenge herself by offering reconciliation only if he will prove his devotion to her by murdering his best friend. He agrees but loses the fight, although his friend Montrose obligingly agrees to pretend death, and the lovers are eventually reconciled. All three plays pose the agonising choice between love and friendship in the most extreme terms possible. In all three cases the man to be killed is the best friend, and in each case the best friend has just won the woman he loves. *A Cure for a Cuckold* even places the duel on his wedding night so that Bonvile's decision is not only a moral but also a sexual one.

However there are significant differences in the ways the three plays formulate the actual condition. In *The Dutch Courtesan* Franceschina clearly names an actual person: she wants the death of Frevil, and hurting Malheureux is only secondary. In *The Parliament of Love*, Leonora just as unambiguously simply wants to punish Claremond. The meaning of Clare's command is far more ambiguous. Although Lessingham does not recognise it at first, it provides him not only with a task to perform but also with a 'riddle' (IV.2.160) to solve. It is the only one of the plays where the command is given in writing: without help from the actions or the tone of voice it is difficult to determine the exact tone or meaning of words. Clare is fond of trying to simplify her own violent and chaotic emotions by reducing them to words on a page: again in IV.2 she can explain her feelings and motives to Bonvile only by handing him a letter.

Throughout the play multiple solutions are suggested for Clare's 'riddle' (IV.2.160). Lessingham from the first suspects she has a 'hidden purpose' (I.2.13), although he is unsure about what it is: perhaps to demonstrate her 'fantasy' (I.2.15) that true friendship can no longer exist in the unheroic modern world. On the whole, however, Lessingham takes her literally, and he does not seriously envisage refusing her command. He is cool and detached about the choice he has to make, imagining rather than feeling 'a brave fight' between 'Love and Friendship' (I.2.29).

In the scene of the duel, Clare's ultimatum is again at the centre of a tissue of double meanings. Bonvile insists that Clare 'does equivocate' (III.1.86), and that her command has a metaphorical rather than a literal meaning:

> Her meaning is, you cherish in your breast
> Either self-love, or pride, as your best friend,
> And she wishes you'd kill that.   (III.1.87–9)

Bonvile's view of his friend here is not altogether an inaccurate one. Lessingham, however, is now convinced that Clare's words should simply be taken literally: 'her command / Is more bloody' (III.1.90–1). In this scene the literal and metaphorical meanings of words collide. Lessingham sees only the literal meanings of words, Bonvile is more alert to their metaphorical undertones. Bonvile insists that he has an advantage in the duel, a 'privy coat' (III.1.101). Lessingham takes this literally until Bonvile explains it as a metaphor for the justice of his cause. Finally Bonvile uses metaphor to save himself from the duel: Lessingham has, metaphorically at least, fulfilled Clare's instructions by killing Bonvile's friendship for him. A duel with words, literal against metaphorical meanings, replaces a duel with weapons. Metaphor is deceptive and mocking, but none the less it leads, tortuously and indirectly, to the happy ending.

Even after the duel scene, a crucial scene for establishing the relationship between literal and metaphorical language, startlingly different solutions are suggested for Clare's riddle. Hearing about the duel, Clare insists that her instructions have been disastrously misinterpreted (III.3.14). Finally she explains her own 'bloody riddle' (III.3.30) by revealing to the amazed Lessingham that her hopeless love for Bonvile had led her to seek her own death. She had thought herself Lessingham's best friend, and hoped to cheat him into killing her, 'unwittingly' (IV.2.79). The play provides multiple solutions, literal or metaphorical, for Clare's riddle: in its confused world any or all of them seems possible. The ambiguous riddle is a powerful image for the play's violent world. Clare and Lessingham are only rescued from the morasse of double-meanings by those whose command of words is more secure than their own, and the happy ending is brought about directly by Bonvile and by Rochfield, and indirectly by Compass.

This tissue of double-meanings and extreme changes of mood is just one aspect of the play's theatrical self-consciousness. In *A Cure for a Cuckold* theatricality seems not only threatening, as it did in *The Devil's Law-case*, but also to be a valid way of expressing feeling and consolidating the happy ending. Compass and Urse stage their own play within the play by separating and rejoining to marry again. Compass like Romelio is surrounded by play-imagery, but unlike Romelio these theatrical undertones do not sabotage but express feeling, and lead not to danger but to the happy ending. Compass objects to losing his wife's child simply because he is not its physical father: 'There's better law among the players yet; for a fellow shall have his share though he do not play that day' (II.3.137–9). In the scene with the lawyers Compass firmly confines violence and immorality to a safely fictional context. Pettifog begins a long and obscene story about an informer infected with the pox by a prostitute. Compass breaks in: 'A Tweak, or Bronstrops – I learned that name in a play' (IV.1.123–4). Rowley makes a good joke by a reference back to his own play, *A Fair Quarrel*, in order to imply the unreality and irrelevance of this fictional background of violence and vice to the comic security of the Compasses. As the play progresses, this admission of theatricality pervades the main plot, and the ending with its extreme poses, abrupt changes of mood, and parodic violence, seems wholly conscious of its own theatricality.

The world of *A Cure for a Cuckold* defines itself through verbal ambiguity, paradox, significantly repeated metaphors, and images of theatricality. In the first four acts the Compass plot predicts a happy ending, but the play's tragicomic progress from metaphorical to literal is a complex one. Act Five is especially rich in its fast-moving interchanges of fiction and fact, which is surprising because by the end of Act Four it looks very much as if metaphor had already been abandoned and as if the happy ending were about to take place. The Compass plot only needs the remarriage festivity to reach its happy ending. Clare's riddle has been solved, and so has Bonvile's as he returns from his metaphorical death. It seems that the surprise we expect in Fletcherian tragicomic endings has been pushed forward into the fourth act. The fifth act, though, finds a new way of treating the tragicomic progress from illusion to reality, and the tragicomic surprise.

Una Ellis-Fermor described *A Cure for a Cuckold* as a moderately successful play 'until frivolous complications of plot and contradictions of character destroy the fifth act'.[6] In the fifth act, indeed, the mode does seem to have changed. It is becoming more blatantly aware of its own theatricality, presenting its extreme antitheses not so much in terms of convincing emotions but in obviously, even parodically, fictional terms. The act develops as a series of emotional scenes played to more moderate audiences, to Annabel, Rochfield, or Woodruff. In the last act of *The Devil's Law-case*, a change in mode distances us from the events of the play and stresses its fictional nature. Actors become audiences, reminding us of our rôle in the dissolving fiction. Comic and ironic overstatement and parody seem to perform the same function in *A Cure for a Cuckold*: the audience is detached from their involvement in the play and compelled to realise its purely fictional nature.

The last scene of the play opens with Annabel's easy tolerance. Although her husband Bonvile has just returned from France and has made no effort to see her, she refuses to believe that this is caused by his 'unkindness' (V.1.9). As a supporter of genuine feeling against the sterile gesture she decides that his 'business' (V.1.12) might be more important than any merely 'formal compliment' (V.1.14) to her. This tolerance, however, is cut across by Lessingham, who enters bringing with him suggestions of tragedy so emphatic and inappropriate as to be touched with parody: 'The ways to love, and crowns, lie both through blood' (V.1.22). The scene sets up the grand gestures of tragedy only to knock them down and to suggest more moderate ways of behaviour.

Lessingham has briefly adopted the role of villainous machiavel and is playing it to the hilt, just too elegantly to be convincing. He copies Iago in his elaborate parturition imagery:[7]

I am grown big with project . . .
A speedy birth fills me with painful throes,

And I am now in labour.   (V.1.25–8)

In a play which has used the imagery of birth and children to express love and reconciliation, and where the comic plot turns on the paternity of a child, Lessingham's exercise in tragic imagery is ironically undermined. We are forced to stop for a minute to consider the relationship between the two plots, and the contrast between Compass's easy forgiveness of his wife and Lessingham's jealous violence. The last act insists on this tragicomic double vision, and despite one or two moments of convincing pain, more and more emphasis is placed on the comic half of the antithesis.

In the final scene the play grotesquely and parodically overstates the theatrical poses of long-suffering wife, jealous husband, and villainous malcontent. Lessingham attempts to push the action over into tragedy as he plans his 'brave revenge' (V.1.37), but the fragility of his assumed character and the tortuously formal language he uses to his Cassio, Rochfield, tip over into parody. Moreover, far from being a credulous victim, Rochfield is fully aware of what is going on, immediately recognising 'some plot to wrong the Bride' (V.1.98) and deliberately misleading the misleader. In the world of the play fictions are benevolent as often as not, and almost every character uses fiction, or fact so tortuously expressed as to be indistinguishable from it.

Lessingham temporarily abandons Iago as his model and begins to act Mephostophilis:[8] 'Of all miseries, I hold that chief, / Wretched to be, when none coparts our grief' (V.1.129–30). He approaches Woodruff with the fiction he has devised, determined to make this work of malice and deceit his 'masterpiece' (V.1.133), like Lodovico in *The White Devil*.[9] He also resumes the equivocating mode which seemed so important earlier in the play, as he speaks again in 'riddles' (V.1.158), informing the uncomprehending Woodruff that Bonvile is at the same time unhurt and 'dangerously wounded' (V.1.150). He goes on to explain this riddle: Bonvile is wounded only metaphorically, 'in his reputation' (V.1.160) by that infidelity of Annabel's which exists only in Lessingham's imagination. Woodruff refuses to believe the story and draws his sword on Lessingham in a parodic version of the duel on Calais sands. Lessingham, whose allegiance to Machiavelli is only skin deep, beats a hasty retreat.

Bonvile now enters, unaware of this latest complication, apparently bringing the happy ending: he seems quite ready to forget the tragicomic disturbances and return to the festivity of the first scene. Woodruff determinedly tones down the tragicomic recriminations and repeats them 'in laughter' (V.1.235). Bonvile, though, is immediately overcome by violent jealousy and suspects his innocent wife. In this scene where characters move between extreme and shifting poses, and where the danger of tragedy is overstated into parody, Bonvile rapidly becomes the jealous and murderous husband.

Suddenly and unexpectedly Clare, who had previously been on the side of anarchy, now becomes the spokesman for the comic ending, as she tries to tell Bonvile the truth and to warn him against his own 'jealousy' (V.1.259). Characters are changing vertiginously, assuming exaggerated conventional rôles and then suddenly inverting them. The penultimate stage of comedy is a period of 'licence and the confusion of values'.[10] Here this is presented in the most extreme and explicit form, affecting background and character, but also pointing forward to the comic festivity. The scene of festivity and reunion becomes a battleground across which Bonvile and Lessingham, Bonvile and Annabel, Clare and Annabel, Bonvile and Woodruff, bicker noisily.

The play returns temporarily to the ambiguous and riddling mode of the early scenes. Bonvile insists that Annabel should return his will, the will which the play has used, like the nuptial carcanet which becomes a fetter, as an image for the changing marriage relationship. Annabel pointedly urges him to give up his 'self-will' (V.1.285), a quibble which echoes the duel scene, where Bonvile himself interprets Clare's riddle as a command to Lessingham to destroy his 'self-love' (III.1.88). It seems we have been swept back into the danger and ambiguity of the play's third act. Bonvile meets Annabel's pun with a quibble of his own, which also echoes a paradox in the third act: he bequeathed his property to her when he was supposed dead, but now that her love for him is really dead, he proposes to have the will altered. The elaborate riddling mode has been resumed, and again leads to misunderstandings which threaten to destroy relationships. This sense of danger, though, is undercut and shortlived. The fact that we as audience know that these fears of infideltiy are baseless, the rapid, balletic changes of combination in the quarrels, and the speed of the untidy exits and entrances, all give the scene a strong leaning towards comedy and parody, which resists the tragicomic danger of riddles and equivocations.

Strangely it is again Clare who takes the first step towards general reconciliation by promising that she will 'solder ... together' (V.1.338) Annabel and Bonvile, even though she was the cause of 'the division' between them (V.1.341). As Romelio the main agent of discord must take the first step towards the happy ending in *The Devil's Law-case*, so Clare, the most confused, passionate and 'lost' of the play's people must become 'the clew. / To lead you forth this labyrinth' (V.1.348–9). Clare, who had previously hidden behind riddles and paradoxes, now explains, clearly and directly, the complicated situation. The play's images of disorientation and the loss of direction are finally righted by Clare's 'clew' and by the 'Compass' who clinches the happy ending. As Clare abandons riddles, Rochfield follows her lead and discards his fictional definitions of his identity by admitting that he approached Annabel not as a lover but as a thief. Complex metaphorical and riddling language reappears only to be discarded as the play finally moves from metaphorical to literal, from fiction to fact.

This change of mood is consolidated by 'soft music' (V.1.437 SD) which is heard and which Bonvile immediately claims as a celebration for the coming wedding of Clare and Lessingham. Immediately the people of the play fit into the patterns of the happy ending under the influence of Compass's wedding music: again Compass's peculiar magic prevails against the forces of violence and disorder, as it did in the scene in which he persuades even the cynical lawyers of his rights in his wife's child. Lessingham apologises to Bonvile for his 'wild distractions' (V.1.441), and promises that he has now controlled his 'fury' (V.1.445). Clare admits that her 'peevish will' (V.1.448) has been to blame and repents. As she and Lessingham quietly accept each other, Lessingham announces the rather subdued happy ending: 'All's now as at first / It was wished to be' (V.1.451–2). The expected love-relationships are finally completed, and the play returns in a circle of disguise, rôle-playing, and riddling language, to the situations and images of its own first act.

However there is still to come the most obvious, and comforting, symbol of the happy ending, as Compass enters with his remarried wife. Compass has embodied the comic spirit throughout the play, and his refusal to accept the conventional theatrical evaluation of the cuckold rebukes the easy jealousy and overstated theatricality of the tragicomic plot. Now that the top plot has crystallised as a consciously theatrical version of experience, the entrance of Compass reduces this plot to a play within the play. In a final tragicomic discord, comedy confronts tragicomedy and reforms it in its own image. As we have come to expect of tragicomedy, the ending of the play sets up a perspective between fiction and the return to real life.

For an instant the two groups hold their positions of extreme contrast, and they then merge as each comments on and accepts the other. The tragicomic synthesis is complete. Compass finally disposes of the danger of the tragicomic plot by his use of death as nothing but a comic metaphor. Woodruff exclaims that Compass is remarrying when his first wife is not yet buried, and Compass agrees: 'No indeed, I mean to dig her grave soon, I have no leisure yet' (V.1.464–5). Frankford is then introduced as 'the father to give the bride' (V.1.479). The baby, actually his natural son, is thus also his 'grandchild' (V.1.481), and also the reborn Compass's elder brother (V.1.483). The riddling mode is resumed but it is no longer a threat, but simply a sign of the metaphorical nature of the play itself and of its comic high-spirits. Finally Compass and Eustace discuss whether a second marriage counteracts or reinforces the first, and the verdict is that 'two affirmatives make no negative' (V.1.494). Rowley's characteristic grammatical joke comments on the play itself. The 'negative' of the tragicomic ending presents us instead with 'two affirmatives', the rebirth and remarriage of Compass, and the education and reconciliation of the young people.

Compass's wedding procession completes the happy ending. At last Woodruff, like Ariosto in *The Devil's Law-case*, comments on this conclusion. The discords which have prepared for the establishment of concord continue to surround the happy ending, not now as a danger, but as a haunting sense of incompleteness:

> Our wedding we have yet to solemnise,
> The first is still imperfect. Such troubles
> Have drowned our music: but I hope all's friends . . .   (V.1.517–19)

Compass speaks the final words of the play, cheerfully riding jokes about cuckoos, and recommending to cuckolds his own stratagem for shedding horns. The broken celebration is resumed, and the play's cyclic form returns to its own beginning.

A Cure for a Cuckold, like *The Devil's Law-case*, presents a disturbing world where equivocation and ambiguity, 'riddles and paradoxes', menace the characters but, unlike *The Devil's Law-case*, a comic subplot establishes early in the play a tolerance and maturity which finally filter through to the tragicomic plot. The two plots, always closely connected by recurring words and images, move closer together in the course of the play until they meet in Act Five. The Compass plot maintains an even comic security, rebuking the violent and passionate characters elsewhere in the play. The tragicomic plot explores convincing pain and isolation but as the play progresses it moves towards deliberate exaggeration, overstatement and frank parody. As in *The Devil's Law-case*, we are progressively distanced from its violence and passion, becoming increasingly aware of its fictional nature as our final detachment from it approaches. *A Cure for a Cuckold* seems a more successful play than most critics have admitted, a play with a firm double-vision which ends in an ironic negation of the tragicomic plot in the form of parody and overstated theatricality, but also in 'two affirmatives' (V.1.494) as comedy and tragicomedy finally synthesise in images of marriage and music.

Conclusion
Music in discord:
John Webster and tragicomedy

Throughout his career John Webster experimented with various ways of ordering extreme contrasts within a single dramatic structure. Beginning his mature career with tragedies which include idle mirth, he ended with formal tragicomedies. All his plays share a desire to juxtapose extremely different episodes, emotions and interpretations.

A particularly important way in which he orders these contrasts is by the use of play images, theatrical allusions and generic terms. *The White Devil* surrounds murder and madness with laughter and comic anecdotes. Its ironic tragedy is built up from allusions to other tragedies: Cornelia is like Ophelia, Florence like Othello, Brachiano like Lear, Vittoria like Agrippina. The play poses tragedy as the climax, a precarious moment of affirmation won from satire at enormous cost. *The Duchess of Malfi* uses a different strategy in its ordering of opposites. The precarious tragic moment is pushed back into the fourth act. Act Four has many of the features we expect of a final act apart from the death of the heroine. Final acts are frequently rich in self-conscious images of the theatre and other arts to mediate for the audience between the world of the play and the real world. Act Four of *The Duchess of Malfi* includes not only an enacted drama, the Masque of Madmen, but also many other images of art: music, 'feign'd statues' (IV.2.351), funerary sculpture, portraits, perspective painting (IV.2.358), actors and acting, 'masque' (IV.2.105) and 'tragedy' (IV.2.8, 36), 'a tedious theatre' (IV.1.84), the audience and its reactions. This act provides a conclusion for the tragedy of the Duchess, but for the unheroic majority the tragic achievement is dissipated in a number of tiny comedies, tragicomedies, parodies of tragedy and reservations about its validity. The great strength of these two plays is that they, in different ways, relate tragedy to other kinds of experience, stressing the ironies that throng around it. Tragedy is placed in the context of 'the Whole Truth'.

133

When his tragedies have these ambiguous qualities, it is not surprising that Webster should have gone on to write formal tragicomedies. In *The Devil's Law-case* and *A Cure for a Cuckold* Webster uses tragicomedy to describe a shifting world of uncertain values, precarious affirmations, and ironic juxtapositions. *A Cure for a Cuckold* is a lively, vivid, compassionate play which parodies the conventions of tragedy. It reaches a secure and moving happy ending through boisterous comedy, 'riddles and paradoxes', unexpected suggestions of romance, and brief but powerful depictions of passion, disorientation and despair. *The Devil's Law-case* is a more challenging play, testing its visual and verbal elements, and presenting a dangerous world not unlike that of the tragedies through inverted conventions and verbal ambiguities. Its ending, where Webster moves from a verbal mode to expression through symbolic action, seems frankly experimental, a convincing evocation of a world of ruined languages where elaborate visual forms are tried out as a way of expressing complicated emotions.

Like the two tragedies, these plays seem particularly interested in their audience. As I have suggested, tragicomedy establishes a close relationship with its audience, defers to them and mocks them, mirrors them in inductions or included plays, uses them as a dramatic character, and forces them to come to terms with their rôle as observers. Almost every event in *The White Devil* has an audience: murders are presented in dumb-shows, the arraignment scene is rich in dramatic quotations, and the entrance of the murderers in Act Five is presented as 'a masque / A matachin' (V.6.169). In *The Duchess of Malfi* Act Four is loaded with theatre images: the Masque of Madmen leads up to murder, and the relationship between audience and actors is reversed as the Duchess watches the masque and then is suddenly involved in her own enactment. A pageant where characters appear in disguise and speak a language recognisably different from the surrounding play is a key episode in the last act of *The Devil's Law-case*, and theatrical parody is an important part of Act Five of *A Cure for a Cuckold*. All these devices suddenly shift our perspectives on the action, and remind us of their fictional nature and of our status as observers.

This consciousness of theatricality is especially significant at the end of tragicomic and near-tragicomic dramas: Act Four of *The Duchess of Malfi* and Act Five of *The White Devil* and *The Devil's Law-case* contain included masques, and Act Five of *A Cure for a Cuckold* is rich in theatrical parody. As fiction gives way to fact, the playwright must help the audience to move back from secondary to primary world. At the end of *Love's Labour's Lost* Armado comments on the unbridgeable gap between play and real life as the fiction ends: 'You that way: we this way' (V.2.923). As *Summer's Last Will and Testament* comes to an end, Will Somers also comments on the separateness of actors and audience by telling us, in Latin to prove his point, that with the ending of the play we can no longer understand him or the language of fiction: '*Barbarus hic ego sum, quia non intelligor ulli*'.[1] These endings mediate for the audience between fiction and real life, commenting on the differences between the two and reminding us that what we have been watching is a dramatic fiction. The tragicomic ending, to use George Eliot's terminology, presents a 'negation', but it is a deliberate negation which tells us not only about the world of the play, but also about the relationship between this fictional world and real life.

John Webster is a much misunderstood dramatist. M. T. Herrick has suggested that of all the great Jacobean playwrights, Webster was the least interested in tragicomedy,[2] while, as I have demonstrated, Webster not only wrote two of the most interesting tragicomedies his age produced, but his tragedies also adapt many of the interests and methods of tragicomedy. Again, it is sometimes suggested that his plays are incoherent or anticlimactic, while I have demonstrated the way ironic repetitions and double images contribute to their coherence, and how tragedy is deliberately placed against a background of different kinds of experience. Finally it is often believed that his latest plays show a sharp decline from the achievement of the tragedies, while it seems to me that they are successful plays in a different mode. Tragedy and idle mirth, terror and laughter, tragic affirmation and an ironic view of this affirmation, a dense verbal texture but also 'grace . . . in action' create these complex plays with their discords and double visions.

Thomas Heywood, perhaps a collaborator with Webster and certainly an innovator in the mixed genres, describes the techniques of his historical writings in his prose work *Gynaikeion* (1624), in which he collects lives of famous women. In imitation of writers for the stage he has, he tells us, intermixed the bare facts of serious history with fiction and even with comedy, 'fabulous Jests and Tales'.[3] He has done this in a deliberate attempt to enrich his historical writings, for 'the most cunning and curious Music is that which is made out of

Discords'. It would be hard to find a more satisfactory description of Webster's tragicomic dramas.

Notes

The place of publication is London, except where otherwise stated.
Publication details are not given here of works included in the bibliography.

Introduction

1 Neil Carson, 'John Webster: the apprentice years' (*The Elizabethan Theatre VI*, ed. G. Hibbard, 1978), p. 76.
2 H. H. Wood (Edinburgh 1934–39) ed., volume III, p. 91.
3 Rupert Brooke, *John Webster and Elizabethan Drama* (1916), p. 75.
4 T. B. Tomlinson, *A Study of Elizabethan and Jacobean Tragedy* (1964), p. 215.
5 M. C. Bradbrook, *Themes and Conventions of Elizabethan Tragedy*, p. 240.
6 Una Ellis-Fermor, *The Jacobean Drama* (1936), p. 183.
7 Madeleine Doran, *Endeavors of Art*, p. 354.
8 Archer in *Nineteenth Century* (vol. 87, no. 515, Jan. 1920), finds the play 'broken-backed'. J. R. Mulryne writes of the 'agreed failure' of the fifth act (*'The White Devil* and *The Duchess Of Malfi'* in *Jacobean Theatre*, Stratford-upon-Avon Studies 1, Brown and Harris eds., 1960, p. 219) and Ian Scott-Kilvert finds it an 'anticlimax' which is 'fatal to the unity of the play' (*John Webster*, 1964, p. 25).

Chapter One

1 Allardyce Nicoll, ' "Tragical-comical-historical-pastoral": Elizabethan dramatic nomenclature' (*Bulletin of the John Rylands Library* 43, 1960–1), p. 70.
2 See Michael Shapiro, 'Audience versus Dramatist in Jonson's *Epicoene* and other plays of the Children's Troupes' (*ELR* III, 1973), pp. 401–17.
3 See Steven C. Young, *The Frame Structure in Tudor and Stuart Drama* (Salzburg 1974).
4 Gregory Smith, *Elizabethan Critical Essays*, vol. 1, 1904, p. 58.
5 *Op. cit.*, p. 59.
6 *Op. cit.*, p. 60.
7 E.g. *1H6* I.4.77, III.1.125, IV.4.7: *2H6* III.1.153, III.2.194, IV.1.4: *3H6* II.3.27, V.6.28: *LLL* V.2.462, V.2.876. Shakespeare uses 'tragedy' ten times, 'tragedies' twice, 'tragic' nine times, 'comedy' ten times. Only two examples come from plays later than *Hamlet*.
8 A. P. Rossiter, *Angel with Horns* (1961), p. 254, describes Shakespeare's use of the words 'tragedy', 'tragic' and 'tragical'.
9 Aristotle, *Poetics* XIII, 11–13.
10 Gregory Smith, *Elizabethan Critical Essays*, vol. 1, 1904, p. 199.
11 F. H. Ristine, *English Tragicomedy, its Origin and History* (New York, 1910).
12 Guarini, *The Compendium of Tragicomic Poetry* (A. H. Gilbert, *Literary Criticism from Plato to Dryden*, 1940), p. 507.

Chapter Two

1 *Measure for Measure* III.1.52.
2 See Michal Shapiro, *Children of the Revels* (New York, 1977) and 'Children's troupes: dramatic illusion and acting style' (*Comparative Drama* III, 1969).
3 Dedications respectively to *The Metamorphosis of Pygmalion's Image*, Book I of *The Scourge of Villainy*, satire XI of *The Scourge*, Book I of *The Scourge*.
4 E. M. Waith, *The Pattern of Tragicomedy in Beaumont and Fletcher* (1952), p. 33.
5 Clifford Leech, *The John Fletcher Plays* (1962), p. 34.
6 Una Ellis-Fermor, *The Jacobean Drama* (1936), p. 205.
7 See, e.g., Peter Davison, 'The serious concerns of *Philaster*' (*ELH* 30, 1963), pp. 1–15, and Arthur Mizener, 'The high design of *A King and No King*' (*MP* 38, 1940–1), pp. 133–54.
8 Ian Fletcher, *Beaumont and Fletcher* (1967), p. 8.
9 See Marco Mincoff, 'Shakespeare, Fletcher and baroque tragedy' (*Sh. Sur.* 20, 1967), pp. 6–7, 14. And see E. M. Waith, 'Characterisation in Fletcher's tragicomedies'.
10 References to *The English Traveller* are from the Mermaid *Thomas Heywood*, ed. A. Wilson Verity (1888).
11 Cinthio, prologue to *Altile*.
12 S. L. Bethell, *Shakespeare and the Popular Dramatic Tradition* (1944), p. 108.
13 References to *Philaster* are from Glover and Waller eds., 1905–12, Cambridge, volume 1.
14 Samuel Schoenbaum, 'The precarious balance of John Marston' (*PMLA* 67, 1952), p. 1070.
15 M. C. Bradbrook, *Themes and Conventions of Elizabethan Tragedy*, p. 247–8.

Chapter Three

1 Joe Lee Davis, *The Sons of Ben* (Detroit 1967), p. 59.
2 Thomas Dekker, *The Guls Horne-booke* (1609), ch. vi.
3 A quotation from Donne, 'The calme', lines 13–14.
4 Arnold Glover, *Beaumont and Fletcher* (Cambridge 1905), volume 1, includes a prose and a verse version of Act V and notes that this act 'is in verse in Quartos A, B, C and D, in prose in Quartos E and F' (p. 433).
5 Glover, *Beaumont and Fletcher* (Cambridge 1905), volume 1, p. xlviii.
6 *Hamlet:* 'prologue' V.2.30; 'play' V.2.31, 199, 245, 276; 'audience' V.2.232, 379; 'stage' V.2.370, 388; 'shows' V.2.394.
7 Frank Kermode, *The Sense of an Ending* (1966), p. 8.
8 Cited by Kermode, *op. cit.*, p. 174.
9 Eric Bentley, *The Life of the Drama* (1965), p. 301.
10 Charles Dickens, *Great Expectations* (1860–1), last sentence of chapter lix.

11 Kermode, *The Sense of an Ending* (1966), p. 175.

Chapter Four

1 Robert Heilman, *Tragedy and Melodrama: Versions of Experience* (Washington 1968), pp. 61–72: Normand Berlin, '*The Duchess of Malfi*: Act V and genre' (*Genre* III, 1970), p. 362: Jane M. Luecke, '*The Duchess of Malfi*: comic and satiric confusion in a tragedy', p. 275.
2 J. R. Mulryne, 'Webster and the uses of tragicomedy', p. 135.
3 Aldous Huxley, 'Tragedy and the whole truth' (*Music at Night* 1931), p. 18.
4 'To the Gentlemen Readers', by R. I., Printer, appended to Octavo and Quarto editions from 1590.
5 Marston, Dedication to *Antonio and Mellida*, line 6.
6 G. Wilson Knight, '*King Lear* and the comedy of the grotesque' (*The Wheel Of Fire*, 1930).
7 Roma Gill, 'A reading of *The White Devil*', p. 42.
8 E. M. Waith, 'Characterisation in John Fletcher's tragicomedies', p. 163.
9 Charles Lamb, 'A note on "The Arraignment of Vittoria" (*The White Devil* III.2)' in *Specimens of the English Dramatic Poets who Lived about the Time of Shakespeare* (included in *John Webster*, G. K. and S. K. Hunter eds., p. 56).
10 R. F. Whitman, *Beyond Melancholy: John Webster and the Tragedy of Darkness* (Salzburg 1972), p. 112.
11 Forty examples of laughter and of the words 'laugh', 'jest', 'smiling', 'merry', 'laughter', 'laughing', 'mirth', 'ridiculous', 'simpers', 'smiles', and 'ridiculously'. This compares with thirty in *The Duchess of Malfi*, twenty-four in *The Devil's Law-case* (including 'pleasant' = 'merry' and 'comical') and twenty in *A Cure for a Cuckold* (including 'pleasant' = 'merry' and 'merrier').
12 Peter Thomson, 'Webster and the actor', p. 41.
13 Thirty references as against forty in *The White Devil*.
14 Ian Scott-Kilvert, *John Webster* (1964), p. 5.

Chapter Five

1 'Plot' V.6.150; 'Act' V.6.294; 'Acted' I.1.31, V.6.131; 'Auditory' III.2.15, V.6.70; 'Perform' II.1.225; 'Part' II.1.225; 'Revels' I.2.80, V.1.53, V.3.8.
2 Echoes *Sejanus* III.1.200–1: 'Is he my accuser? / And must he be my judge?'
3 Cf. *Sejanus* IV.1.1–2: 'You must have patience, royal Agrippina. / I must have vengeance first.'
4 Cf. *The Atheist's Tragedy* I.4.123–6: 'A rape, a rape, a rape! . . . Why, what is't but a rape to force a wench / To marry?'
5 Cf. Holinshed, *Chronicles* (1587), iii 908/2/2 (cit. W. G. Boswell-Stone, *Shakespeare's Holinshed* (1896), p. 468).

6   *King Lear* IV.6.89–90, III.4.32–3.
7   Cf. *WD* III.2.138–9: 'I scorn to hold my life / At yours or any man's entreaty.'
8   'Noble' V.6.120, III.2.54; 'Charity' III.2.161; 'Pity' V.6.183; 'Merciful' I.1.57; 'Goodness' V.6.269; 'Honour' I.2.308; 'Holy' III.2.77; 'Penitence' V.3.252; 'Virtue' I.1.50.

Chapter Six

1   William Archer, review of 1919 production of *Malfi*, *Nineteenth Century* (vol. 87, no. 515, Jan. 1920): Ian Scott-Kilvert, *John Webster* (1964), p. 25.
2   C. G. Thayer, 'The ambiguity of Bosola', p. 168, 170.
3   Dorothea Krook, *Elements of Tragedy*, pp. 8–9.
4   Sidney, *Arcadia* V (*Works* II.177): 'in such a shadow, or rather pit of darkness, the wormish mankind lives . . .'.
5   Introduction to *The Faithful Shepherdess*, Glover and Wallace, (Cambridge 1906), volume II, p. 522.

Chapter Seven

1   Ralph Berry, *The Art of John Webster* (1972), p. 165.
2   Madeleine Doran, *Endeavors of Art*, p. 354.
3   Northrop Frye, 'The argument of comedy', p. 58.
4   D. C. Gunby, '*The Devil's Law-case*: an interpretation', p. 558.
5   Doran, *op. cit.*
6   F. L. Lucas, *The Complete Works of John Webster* (1927), vol. 2, p. 224.
7   Sydney Anglo, *Spectacle, Pageantry and Tudor Policy* (1969), p. 177.

Chapter Eight

1   Inga-Stina Ewbank, 'Webster's constructional rhythm', pp. 165–76.
2   For a discussion of the stylistic features of Rowley's work see Dewar M. Robb, 'The canon of William Rowley's plays', pp. 129–41.
3   E.g. H. D. Gray, '*A Cure for a Cuckold* by Heywood, Webster and Rowley' (*MLR* 22, 1927), pp. 389–97.
4   See C. J. Sisson, *Lost Plays of Shakespeare's Age* (Cambridge 1936), pp. 80–124.
5   Beatrice, of course, derives from 'beata', and is the name of the 'blessed' woman who is Dante's guide in Paradise, while Joanna (Juana) was the name of a mad Spanish queen (1492–1555): an interesting link between the heroine and the madhouse plot.
6   Una Ellis-Fermor, *The Jacobean Drama* (1936), p. 183.
7   cf. *Othello* I.3.401, II.1.127–8.
8   Cf. *Dr Faustus* I.5.42.
9   *The White Devil* V.6.299.
10 Northrop Frye, 'The argument of Comedy', p. 67.

Conclusion

1 'I am a barbarian here, because I am not understood by anybody' (*The Unfortunate Traveller and Other Works*, 1972, ed. J. B. Steane, p. 207).
2 M. T. Herrick, *Tragicomedy*, p. 280.
3 Thomas Heywood, *Gunaikeion: or Nine Books of Various History Concerning Women* . . . (1624). Epistle 'To the Reader' A4*v*.
4 Thomas Heywood, *op. cit.*

Abbreviations

ELH	*English Literary History*
ELR	*English Literary Renaissance*
E&S	*Essays and Studies*
JEGP	*Journal of English and Germanic Philology*
MLQ	*Modern Language Quarterly*
MLR	*Modern Language Review*
MP	*Modern Philology*
N&Q	*Notes and Queries*
PMLA	*Publications of the Modern Language Association of America*
PQ	*Philological Quarterly*
RES	*Review of English Studies*
SEL	*Studies in English Literature*
Sh. Sur.	*Shakespeare Survey*
SP	*Studies in Philology*

Cure	*A Cure for a Cuckold*
DLC	*The Devil's Law-case*
Malfi	*The Duchess of Malfi*
WD	*The White Devil*

SOED	*Shorter Oxford English Dictionary*

Editions used

In the case of editions in old-style spelling, I have modernised spelling. In the case of *The White Devil* I have chosen to disagree with John Russell Brown and follow the Quarto spelling of the name Brachiano.

Webster
The White Devil, J. R. Brown, 1960 (The Revels Plays)
The Duchess of Malfi, J. R. Brown, 1964 (The Revels Plays)
The Devil's Law-case, Elizabeth Brennan, 1975 (New Mermaid)
A Cure for a Cuckold, F. L. Lucas, *The Complete Works of John Webster*, vol. III (1927)

Beaumont and Fletcher
A King and No King, R. K. Turner jr., 1964 (Regents Renaissance Drama)
Other plays, Glover and Waller eds., Cambridge, 1905–12

Marston
The Malcontent, A. H. Gomme, *Jacobean Tragedies* (1969)
The Dutch Courtesan, Martin Wine, 1965 (Regents Renaissance Drama)
Antonio and Mellida, G. K. Hunter, 1965 (Regents Renaissance Drama)
Antonio's Revenge, W. Reavley Gair, 1978 (The Revels Plays)
Other plays, H. H. Wood, Edinburgh 1934–9
Poems, Arnold Davenport, Liverpool, 1961

Marlowe
The Complete Plays, J. B. Steane ed., 1969 (Penguin)

Massinger
Plays and Poems of Philip Massinger, P. Edwards and C. Gibson eds., Oxford 1976

Shakespeare
The Complete Works, Peter Alexander ed., 1951

Ben Jonson
Herford and Simpson, 1925–52

Ford
Henry Weber ed., *Dramatic Works of John Ford* (1811)

Sir William Alexander
Works, vol. 1, ed., L. E. Kastner and H. B. Charlton, Edinburgh 1921

Parnassus Plays
J. B. Leishman ed., 1949

The Spanish Tragedy
Philip Edwards ed., 1959 (The Revels Plays)

A Warning for Fair Women
Tudor Facsimile Text, 1912, John S. Farmer ed.

The Antipodes
Anne Haaker ed., 1967 (Regents Renaissance Drama)

Locrine
C. F. Tucker Brooke, *The Shakespeare Apocrypha* (Oxford 1908)

Soliman and Perseda
F. S. Boas, *The Works of Thomas Kyd* (Oxford 1901)

Lyly's *Campaspe*
Malone Society Reprint, *Alexander and Campaspe*, W. W. Greg ed., 1933.

Tudor Tragicomedies

Apius and Virginia, Peter Happé, *Tudor Interludes* (1972)

Damon and Pythias, Malone Society Reprint, eds. A. Brown and F. P. Wilson, 1957

The Glass of Government, J. W. Cunliffe, *The Complete Works of Gascoigne* (1907–10)

The Virtuous Octavia, Malone Society Reprint, ed. R. B. McKerrow, 1909

Except where otherwise stated, dates of plays are taken from Harbage, *Annals of English Drama* (revised by S. Schoenbaum, 1964)

Select bibliography

General

S. L. Bethell, *Shakespeare and the Popular Dramatic Tradition* (1944)
M. C. Bradbrook, *Themes and Conventions of Elizabethan Tragedy* (Cambridge 1935)
Madeleine Doran, *Endeavors of Art* (Madison 1954)
Una Ellis-Fermor, *The Jacobean Drama* (1936)
Frank Kermode, *The Sense of an Ending* (1966)
Dorothea Krook, *Elements of Tragedy* (New Haven 1969)
Anne Righter, *Shakespeare and the Idea Of The Play* (1962)

Comedy and Satire

C. L. Barber, *Shakespeare's Festive Comedy* (Princeton 1959)
Anne Barton, '*As You Like It* and *Twelfth Night*: Shakespeare's sense of an ending' (Stratford-upon-Avon Studies 14, *Shakespearian Comedy*, Bradbury and Palmer eds., 1972), pp. 160–80.
Northrop Frye, 'The argument of comedy' (*English Institute Essays* 1948), pp. 58–73.
———, *A Natural Perspective* (1965)

Tragicomedy and Beaumont and Fletcher

Philip Edwards, 'The danger not the death: the art of John Fletcher' (Stratford-upon-Avon Studies 1, *Jacobean Theatre* Brown and Harris eds., 1960), pp. 159–77.
P. J. Finkelpearl, 'Beaumont, Fletcher, and 'Beaumont And Fletcher': some distinctions' (*ELR* 1, 1971), pp. 144–64.
M. T. Herrick, *Tragicomedy: its Origin and Development in Italy, France and England* (Urbana 1955).
Clifford Leech, *The John Fletcher Plays* (1962).
F. H. Ristine, *English Tragicomedy, its Origin and History* (New York 1910).
E. M. Waith, 'Characterisation in John Fletcher's tragicomedies' (*RES* 19, 1943), pp. 141–64.
———, *The Pattern of Tragicomedy in Beaumont and Fletcher* (New Haven 1952).

Marston

J. Scott Colley, ' "Opinion" and the reader in John Marston's *The Metamorphosis of Pygmalion's Image*' (*ELR* 3, 1973), pp. 221–31.
P. J. Finkelpearl, *John Marston of the Middle Temple* (Cambridge, Mass. 1969).
R. A. Foakes, 'John Marston's fantastical plays, *Antonio and Mellida* and *Antonio's Revenge*' (*PQ* 41, 1962), pp. 229–37.

G. K. Hunter, 'English folly and Italian vice' (Stratford-upon-Avon Studies 1, *Jacobean Theatre*, Brown and Harris eds., 1960), pp. 85–111.
——, Regents Renaissance editions of *Antonio and Mellida* (1965) and *Antonio's Revenge* (1966).

Webster (general)

Ralph Berry, *The Art of John Webster* (1972).
Travis Bogard, *The Tragic Satire of John Webster* (New York 1955).
R. W. Dent, *John Webster's Borrowing* (Berkeley 1960).
J. R. Mulryne, 'Webster and the uses of tragicomedy' (*John Webster*, Brian Morris ed., 1970), pp. 133–55.
P. B. Murray, *A Study of John Webster* (The Hague 1969).
Hereward T. Price, 'The function of imagery in Webster' (*PMLA* 70, 1955), pp. 717–39.
Peter Thomson, 'Webster and the actor' (*John Webster*, Brian Morris ed., 1970), pp. 23–44.

The White Devil

Anders Dalby, *The Anatomy of Evil: a study of John Webster's The White Devil* (Malmö 1974).
Roma Gill, 'A reading of *The White Devil*' (*E&S* 19, 1966), pp. 41–59.
J. R. Hurt, 'Inverted rituals in Webster's *The White Devil*' (*JEGP* 61, 1962), pp. 42–7.
B. J. Layman, 'The equilibrium of opposites in *The White Devil*' (*PMLA* 74, 1959), pp. 336–47.

The Duchess of Malfi

David Bergeron, 'The wax figures in *The Duchess of Malfi*' (*SEL* 18, 1978), pp. 331–9.
Normand Berlin, '*The Duchess of Malfi*: Act V and genre' (*Genre* 1970), pp. 351–63.
Inga-Stina Ekeblad, 'The "Impure Art" of John Webster' (*RES* n.s. vol 9, 1958), pp. 253–67.
——, 'A Webster's villain: a study of character imagery in *The Duchess of Malfi*' (*Orpheus* 3, 1956), pp. 126–33.
Louis D. Gianetti, 'A contemporary view of *The Duchess of Malfi*' (*Comparative Drama* 3, winter 1969–70), pp. 297–307.
Jane M. Luecke, '*The Duchess of Malfi*: comic and satiric confusion in a tragedy' (*SEL* 4, 1964), pp. 275–90.
Joyce E. Peterson, *Curs'd Example: The Duchess of Malfi and Commonweal Tragedy* (Columbia, 1978)
C. G. Thayer, 'The ambiguity of Bosola' (*SP* 54, 1957), pp. 167–71.

The Devil's Law-case

Lee Bliss, 'Destructive will and social chaos in *The Devil's Law-case*' (*MLR* 72, 1977), pp. 513–25.

Gunnar Boklund, '*The Devil's Law-case*: an end or a beginning?' (*John Webster*, Brian Morris ed., 1970), pp. 115–30.

D. C. Gunby, '*The Devil's Law-case*: an interpretation' (*MLR* 63, 1968), pp. 545–58.

A Cure for a Cuckold

Inga-Stina Ewbank, 'Webster's constructional rhythm' (*ELH* 24, 1957), pp. 165–76.

H. D. Gray, '*A Cure for a Cuckold* by Heywood, Webster and Rowley' (*MLR* 22, 1927), pp. 389–97.

Dewar M. Robb, 'The canon of William Rowley's plays' (*MLR* 45, 1950), pp. 129–41.

H. D. Sykes, 'Webster's share in *A Cure for a Cuckold*' (*N&Q* 9, 1914), pp. 382–4, 404–5, 443–5, 463–4.

Index